HOW TO PUBLISH YOURSELF

HOW TO PUBLISH YOURSELF

Peter Finch

a&b

This edition published in Great Britain in 1997 by
Allison & Busby Ltd
114 New Cavendish Street
London W1M 7FD

First published in Great Britain in 1987 by Allison & Busby
an imprint of Wilson & Day Ltd

A catalogue record for this book is available from
the British Library.

ISBN 0 74900 301 4

Designed and typeset by N-J Design Associates
Romsey, Hampshire
Printed and bound in Great Britain by
WBC Book Manufacturers
Bridgend, Mid Glamorgan

CONTENTS

Acknowledgements

Introduction

1 You want to publish yourself   1
2 There's nothing new in this   6
3 The present scene   13
4 It can be done – present-day successes   19
5 How to set yourself up   27
6 What does a book look like?   38
7 Getting it together – the presentation of copy   45
8 The printing process   53
9 Design   59
10 How to make it cheaper   67
11 Proceeding upwards – how to improve   77
   on the basics
12 Can't cope?   83
13 Desktop publishing is no such thing   88
14 Selling   93
15 Marketing and promotion   105
16 It doesn't have to be a book   114
17 Poetry: a special case   123
18 If it can go wrong, it will   128

Appendix One: 134
Organisations of Interest to Self-publishers

Appendix Two: 137
Books of Interest to Self-publishers

Index   141

ACKNOWLEDGEMENTS

Unless otherwise stated, remarks in this book attributed to specific writers were made to the author in the course of his researches. Other copyright quotations come from the following, to whom full acknowledgement is made:

Bill Adler: *Inside Publishing*, Bobbs-Merrill. B. E. Bellamy: *Private Presses and Publishing in England Since 1945*, Clive Bingley. Anthony Blond: *The Book Book*, Jonathan Cape. Brian Cookman: *Desktop Design*, Blueprint. e. e. cummings: *Collected Poems*, Harcourt Brace Jovanovich, Inc. Jane Dorner: *Writing on Disk*, John Taylor Book Ventures. Bill Henderson: *The Publish-It-Yourself Handbook*, Pushcart. David Hewson: from *The Wordsmith*, Issue One, Jan/Feb 1986, Mandarin Publishing. Norman Hidden: *How to Be Your Own Publisher*, Workshop Press. Roy Lewis and John B. Easson: *Printing and Publishing at Home*, David & Charles. Anais Nin: *In Praise of the Sensitive Man*, W. H. Allen. Peter Owen (editor): *Publishing Now*, Peter Owen. Victor Papanek: *Design for the Real World*, Thames and Hudson. Will Ransom: *Private Presses and Their Books*, Philip C. Duschnes. Herbert Simon: *Introduction to Printing*, Faber & Faber. Gertrude Stein: *How To Write*, Something Else Press. Sir Stanley Unwin: *The Truth About A Publisher*, George Allen & Unwin. Audrey and Philip Ward: *The Small Publisher*, Oleander Press.

INTRODUCTION

How to Publish Yourself is the result of a number of years spent doing just that. I began as a self-publisher and my first three booklets of poems were all examples of doing-it-myself. Their appearance led to enquiries from friends as to how I'd gone about it and how much it had all cost. Later, when I expanded my publishing operations to include the literary journal *Second Aeon*, I found myself an unwitting fount of information for aspiring creative writers from all over. 'Well, how do you do it?' I'd be asked and I'd have to tell. As treasurer of the Association of Little Presses I was flooded with requests for help, usually by phone. People would ring up at 9.00 p.m. on a Sunday, just as I was off to the pub, wanting to know if I could recommend a distributor for the 500-page collection of Cotswold train-spotting anecdotes they'd just brought out. Now, as manager of a bookshop, I meet customers personally. They all want to know if I think they should go ahead. I tell them yes.

It is obvious there should be a simple, accessible guide for all these individuals and groups who want to publish on their own. Many have decided to bring out a booklet simply for reasons of self-satisfaction, while others launch their title as a prelude to bigger things. Self-publishing does not have to be a complex process, as *How to Publish Yourself* will show; the pitfalls are marked and the rewards indicated; and stories of self-publishers, past and present, are included as inspirational examples. Vitally important, of course, I no longer need explain myself at length – Sunday evenings free again: I simply point to the book.

Most gratifyingly the first edition of *How to Publish Yourself* resulted in a steady stream of letters from those who had followed its advice and gone on to do it themselves. Local guidebooks acquired ISBNs and entered the bookstores; pamphlets of poetry got reviewed where they were formerly ignored; autobiographies were hardbacked without bankrupting their authors; a fabulous tale of wartime escape from Austria went into multiple editions; a multilingual phrasebook for lovers was splashed by the nationals and sold into the chains. Better still, at my own bookshop, I began to detect the book's advice being used against me. Self-publishers who'd got their costings right and included a title on their spines rang the right numbers on the right days and actually got me to buy their works; others entered quietly at lunchtimes and surreptitiously rearranged my displays. Self-publishing was on the up.

This second edition of *How to Publish Yourself*, which you hold now, has been completely revised and comprehensively rewritten. Trades shift and technologies, especially those pertaining to printing, move on at a considerable pace. The work – both the original composition and the subsequent rewrite – has involved a considerable amount of enquiry. I'd like to thank the many small and self-publishers who responded to my requests for information, filled in my questionnaires and sent me samples of their books. Not every tale is retold – there are too many – but it is undoubtedly an inspiration for those at the point of starting to learn that there are so large a number who have already taken the plunge. Appreciation should also be expressed to the firms, companies, corporations, societies, boards, libraries, organisations and associations who took the trouble to advise me. I'd especially like to thank Gordon Wells who kept me supplied with cuttings, my friend Ron Knowles who spent a considerable amount of time hunting out references and turning up ideas, Keith James who patiently answered my queries on design, Huw James who helped by explaining small business financing, Mick Felton who advised on specialist publishing, Sue Wilshere who read a number of my drafts and my children who were denied the occasion to speak to me, even on the phone, for some time.

How to Publish Yourself doesn't answer everything – it isn't big enough. But there is enough information here to turn most readers into publishers, if that is what they want. It doesn't matter, either, if everyone begins at once. In publishing there is room for all.

Peter Finch
Caerdydd, 1998

1

YOU WANT TO PUBLISH YOURSELF

So you want to publish yourself? Is it really possible? Isn't publishing actually in the same league as motorway construction, Channel Tunnel digging or satellite launching? You could make it so. If this were 1935 and you were Allen Lane starting the paperback revolution with the first Penguin you might be facing problems of some complexity. Thankfully, bringing out a single edition of your own book is much simpler than that.

To many of us publishing is an arcane art. The issuing of works – literary or otherwise – in multiple copies and the causing of them to be put on sale seem both mysterious and difficult. Yet in reality the process is not that complicated. If you take time out to understand the general principles, publishing can be made as easy as you want it to be. This book will attempt to show you how.

Can you do it?

So it might be possible, but that doesn't make it ethical. Isn't there an element of deception in this? Won't other people be suspicious if they find out that the publisher of a book is also its author?

> Writers imagine that they must be commercially published in order to be proud of their work. "If my manuscript is worthwhile, why didn't a commercial house accept it?" The myth persists.
> Bill Henderson

At the end of the day it is a matter of conditioning. Most of us imagine the imprint of a respected commercial publisher to be the only way to lend authority to a work, but this does not have to be the case. Ever since publishing began, there have been enough enterprising self-publishers around to undermine totally the idea that books can be desirable only if they are brought out by an independent intermediary. If you believe in what you've done strongly enough then why not back your own judgement and self-publish? That would be a perfectly ethical act. And as to deluding others – not at all. It is the work which is important, what your book says and does, rather than the imprint on the spine.

1

Why do it?

> It is an evasion of the whole question just to put it down to vanity.
>
> Howard Sergeant

It is perhaps well to sort out your reasons before you begin:

1   You've tried commercial publishers and you've been rejected. The most common of reasons and nothing to be ashamed of. It is worth remembering that James Joyce's *Dubliners* was turned down by twenty-two publishers and J. P. Donleavy's *The Ginger Man* came back thirty-six times.

2   What you've written is not in an accepted commercial format, or so you've been told. It's too short or too long; it's a pamphlet of poems and no one does pamphlets; it's a collection of short stories and no one publishes collections; it's a novella and novellas never sell. You may be puzzled by this and point out examples of all three formats in your local bookshop. If you ask you'll be told that these are the *exceptions* while in your case the publishers are sticking to the rules.

3   What you have produced is of such *local* interest – a guidebook, a town history, the story of a sports club – that no publisher exists who is willing to enter such a narrow market.

4   It is so specialised or technical – a book about swimming-pool tiles or a survey of grub-screws – that no commercial publisher can identify a market for it.

5   You want to do it yourself for artistic reasons. You are an experimental poet fond of typography or a novelist wedded to the idea of purple paper and you wish complete control of the publishing processes.

6   What you've written takes political risks. It is *agitprop*, a challenge to some established part of the system or an attack on commerce. You'd rather do it yourself than go through regular channels.

7   You need a publication out very quickly, perhaps as a qualifier for a job or to provide eligibility for entrance to a scheme such as *Writers on Tour*. Commercial publishers take years. You cannot wait that long.

8   You want to take up small publishing as a hobby and decide that your first author ought to be yourself.

9 You've seen a gap in the market, as Michael Pandya did with his handbook on Indian curries, and make a business decision to fill it.

10 You have an idea for a film or TV series and decide that the best way of selling it to the producers is to have it published in the form of a book.

11 You have a publisher but your latest work has been rejected on the grounds that it is somehow unsuitable. You decide that your publisher is wrong.

12 You resent the money made by publishers, apparently out of their authors, and decide you can do better on your own.

Keep in mind why you are self-publishing. It will affect many of the decisions you'll now have to make.

What goes best?

Absolutely anything can be self-published. In a range that starts with a postcard view of a local harbour and ends at a multi-volume encyclopaedia there are countless examples of writers who have gone it alone. It has to be said, though, that some things are easier than others. Complex many-illustrated works involving full-colour process and varied typesetting are both costly and technically demanding to produce. Self-published novels, while pretty straightforward to produce, can prove a much tougher prospect when it comes to selling. Poetry is easiest when it comes to production, not outrageously expensive, but still hard to shift. Local history, so long as the photographs, maps and illustrations are handlable, always has a ready market. Anything specialist where the self-publisher is an expert and the knowledge is sought after will work. A vast family history will circulate only among the family. A book of short stories will prove almost impossible to sell. But don't let me put you off too early. There are exceptions to everything. If you want to self-publish then do so, but do take care.

How complex is it?

Your job isn't over when you finish writing the book. It has just started.

US authors' agent, Bill Adler

3

Just how complex is publishing? How skilled do you have to be? The answer to that is really for you to decide. You can sit at your desk and pay for it all to be done for you. Financiers do this with the ghosted auto-biographies they bring out and which nobody reads. Or at the other extreme you can roll up your sleeves and learn the whole craft and, like William Blake before you, become involved in every process there is.

But for an average person wanting average involvement, what is required?

● Some skill with words. But you'll have that because you are a writer.

● Some knowledge of books. What they look like, where to get them, and who uses them and a realistic notion of how many of these people there are.

● A facility with paper. An eye for straight lines, a liking for neatness, a feeling for shapes and form.

● A bit of chat. If you are completely retiring then someone else will have to handle the marketing and that is at least half of what publishing is.

● Finally, patience. Whatever the project is, and no matter how much quicker the self-publisher can get it done, it will still take time.

Not too much time, though. You could run it all out of a briefcase in a bed-sit if you wanted to. But if you do decide to get further into it, what is expected? How skilled need you become? To answer that you really need to know a bit more about what publishers, printers, authors and booksellers actually are. Some publishers are also printers, like Oxford University Press; some printers occasionally publish. A few booksellers are run by publishers – OUP has its own store; while others – W. H. Smith, for instance – have been known to bring out their own books. There can be authors involved in all three professions. The norm, however, is for all the processes to be entirely independent and completely distinct.

It wasn't always like this. In the early days of Caxton and his assistant, Wynkyn de Worde, the type-founder, printer, binder, editor, publisher and bookseller were often the same person. With the coming of the industrial revolution the functions separated and it is now possible to see almost every aspect of every process in the production and selling of books carried out by different firms. Today printing is a most post-industrial activity. To quote Anthony Blond, 'the modern compositor (typesetter) wears an M. & S. cashmere woolly and has clean fingernails; his grandad was inky-fingered in an overall.'

The amount of skill you need will depend of how many of the numerous aspects of the process you decide to tackle yourself. Some are reasonably simple and require no more than dexterity and practice – perfect home-binding perhaps, or paste-up. Others can only be learned by apprenticeship – cloth casing or the complexities of the four-colour process. Yet again much depends on how much equipment you own or are prepared to buy. Many small home-publishers and enthusiasts do their own finishing (that's pulling all the printed pages and covers together to form the book) which requires little space or capital. Yet few, if any, have invested in a web-fed multi-litho in order to print just one or two books. I must stress than none of this is obligatory. In publishing, especially small-scale self-publishing, if you do not have aptitude or inclination for a particular process then you can always employ someone else to do it for you.

Time is an important factor. Commercial publishing is not geared to instant or even quickly produced books. There are exceptions, for example paperbacks on the raid at Entebbe and the Gulf War, which reached the shops almost before the events themselves had drawn to a close. As a rule, though, publishing is a drawn-out procedure. Michael Legat, in his excellent *Authors' Guide to Publishing* (Hale), reckons that the normal publishing process from acceptance of a finished typescript to publication takes about nine months. The self-publisher need suffer from no such constraints. The production time depends on the size and complexity of the job in hand, but assuming that the book is reasonably straightforward and that you are paying for most of the aspects of production to be carried out rather than doing them yourself, a time span of six weeks would be reasonable. Even if you were self-sufficient and did everything from typesetting to binding yourself you could still cut a fair bit off nine months. Doing it yourself puts you in charge: you decide priorities; you decide how things get done.

There is little to becoming a self-publisher: no exams, no qualifications, no bureaucracy, no registration. Only will and application. Technology has advanced wonderfully. Everybody can be their own publisher now.

2

THERE'S NOTHING NEW IN THIS

Self-publishing has been around since Gutenberg first moved a type. It is an honourable tradition. In the early days of print authors had really little to gain from being published. They were not paid and nor were their names included anywhere on the book. Only the printer, if he remembered, got an acknowledgement and that at the end of the text. With the adoption of title pages, the situation changed and the names of both writer and publisher began to appear. Books were turning into business. Yet despite printer's and publisher's profits, authors remained largely unpaid. What was of upmost importance was the text, and as late as 1750 it was still considered unseemly to write for remuneration rather than reputation. Very few writers received money from their publishers and those who did kept the fact well hidden.

By the beginning of the nineteenth century there was a slight improvement when changes in the copyright law eventually provided writers with something they could sell. It became common for authors to contribute financially towards the publication of their books, taking a share in profits if there were any. Countless authors worked in this fashion, including many pre-eminent in their day. Charles Dickens financed *A Christmas Carol*, paying Chapman & Hall the complete production costs and accepting sales income less publishers' commission. In 1811, Thomas Egerton published Jane Austen's *Sense and Sensibility*, standing all costs but making sure, by contractual arrangement, that 'the authoress was to reimburse him for any loss'. By the time John Murray had become her publisher, Jane Austen was actually paying herself. She financed production of both *Mansfield Park* and *Emma*, taking all profits less her publishers' 10 per cent. It is interesting to record that John Murray, along with one or two other London publishers, occasionally still operates in this fashion.

Sponsorship varies from book to book. Sometimes the publisher takes no financial risk; more often the cost is shared with the author or, as in the case of company histories, a large firm sale for the title is agreed in advance. I would not like to give the impression that the arrangement is a common twentieth-century practice, but it does happen.

With the passing of the 1911 Copyright Act, the concept of the writer producing something of a value which could be leased or sold

6

became firmly established. Writers began to be paid in proportion to their sales, by royalty. Compared to past practice this was a breakthrough, yet it did not signal the demise of the self-publisher. Like the population from which they were drawn, authors were on the increase. There was greater call than ever for publication and commercial publishers were both unable and unwilling to cope. Self-publishing, if clandestine, became commonplace. As novelist Jack Trevor Story remarked, 'Only history has let the cat out of the bag.' Horace Walpole, William Makepeace Thackeray, Honoré de Balzac, Walt Whitman, Virginia Woolf, Gertrude Stein, John Galsworthy, Rudyard Kipling, Beatrix Potter, Thomas Paine, Lord Byron, Edward Fitzgerald (*The Rubáiyát of Omar Khayyám*), Mark Twain, Edwin Arlington Robinson, Upton Sinclair, W. H. Davies, Zane Grey, Carl Sandburg, William Carlos Williams and many others all at some stage in their careers self-published. They are clearly among literature's long-term successes: we still recognise their names.

When examined, the reasons these writers chose to self-publish will usually be found to apply still today. There have been few changes, save in technology – and more of that anon.

Money has traditionally been at the root of many a writer's misgivings about the system and self-publishing offers a way of gaining better returns. In 1790, Alexander Pope made an amazing £5,320 from his self-published English translation of Homer's *Iliad*, a popular work for which the author correctly forecast a large demand. Sixty-six years later, Robert Burns needed to make only nine guineas, the price of a passage to Jamaica. He was surrounded by problems, including a pregnant woman who refused to marry him, and had decided that the best way out was to flee. At his landlord's suggestion, he attempted to raise the ticket money by bringing out a book of his poems and selling it to friends and neighbours. He used a Kilmarnock jobbing printer to produce *Poems, Chiefly in the Scottish Dialect*. The venture worked. Burns had had the forethought to collect 350 advance orders, enough to finance the project completely. The edition ran to 614 copies and was such a success that Burns forgot Jamaica and moved to Edinburgh where a second edition netted a further profit of £500.

The system of collecting orders for books before publication, selling by *subscription*, was common among publishers in the eighteenth century. It is still a useful technique today. Those lucky enough to own a first edition of Philip Larkin's collection *The Less Deceived* (published by Marvel Press in 1955) will notice that it contains the names of all those who paid in advance and thereby ensured production.

John Ruskin turned to self-publishing in the 1870s with his *Fors Clavigera* – a series of essays directed at the labourers of Great Britain. He did so in part to avoid censorship but mainly as a protest against the huge profits being made by publishers and booksellers. His ideas were a foreshadowing of 1960s alternative society. He wanted to publish and sell entirely on his terms. No one would be exploited.

The altruism of Ruskin and his assistant George Allen went completely against the commercialism of the day. There was no advertising, no promotion, no complimentaries and no review copies. The books were priced at sixpence a copy, plus a penny postage. No discounts. If you wanted the book, this was what you had to pay. This remarkable system also applied to booksellers, which was an unfortunate move. Ruskin wanted the public to know what they were getting, if anyone was making a profit out of them and if so by how much. Those with an interest in retailing *Fors Clavigera* were therefore obliged to charge an amount equivalent to their usual profit margin on top. There were complaints which multiplied when it was discovered that Ruskin was also busy commending his scheme to others. A booksellers' boycott was only partially successful since preventing Ruskin from appearing on shop shelves did not stop the public coming in and asking for his books, obliging the booksellers to abandon their boycott.

Ruskin was an idealist, convinced that what he had to say must stand or fall on its worth alone. *Fors Clavigera* was against competition and self-interest and a promoter of heroic, feudal and Christian social ideals. The whole project should have ended in disaster yet in the event again proved the efficacy of self-publishing by becoming a success. Ruskin, if not made rich, at least made money. His assistant went on to found the commercial publishers George Allen & Unwin.

Like Ruskin, a number of authors have been prompted to self-publish as a way of getting round the restrictions of the day. It bothered James Joyce very early in his career that his essay 'The Day of the Rabblement' should be rejected from his college magazine simply because it referred to a book listed on the Vatican's index of proscribed works. Determined not to be silenced, he teamed up with fellow student Francis Skeffington, whose essay on equal status for women had been similarly censored. Using the college printer, they jointly brought out *Two Essays* in an edition of eighty-five copies, at total cost of £2 5s. Distribution of such a small run posed few difficulties and drew far more attention to the essays than would have been the case had they appeared lost in the vast contents of the magazine to which they had originally been sent.

University was also the location for Shelley's venture into self-publishing. His provocatively titled *The Necessity of Atheism* was brought out in 1811, using an Oxford printer and advertised in the local paper as 'to be had of booksellers of London and Oxford'. As is often the case with such hopeful announcements this proved to be an exaggeration. Shelley's subject matter was so controversial for the day that no bookseller, local or otherwise, would handle it.

The poet was forced to pioneer a technique now common among small-press operators and many well-known authors. He entered the premises of booksellers Munday & Slatter while the principals were at lunch and, telling the shop assistant that all had been previously arranged, proceeded to scatter copies throughout the store. Caught up in the spirit of things he also built a window display which proved to be his undoing. It was spotted almost immediately by a passing clergyman. An incensed Reverend John Walker complained so vociferously to the booksellers that the offending works were straight away removed and burned in the bookshop's kitchen stove. Undaunted, Shelley sent copies of what he had left to the Bishop of Oxford, to the Chancellor of the University and to the master of every college. There was outrage, with the inevitable result. Within a day Shelley, alias Jeremiah Stukeley under whose name the works had been published, was found out, sent for by the Dean of his college, and expelled.

D. H. Lawrence had long dallied with the idea of self-publishing as a way to avoid censorship, in his case suppression on moral rather than religious grounds. In 1916, he had tried to found Rainbow Books and Music in order to bring out his controversial book *The Rainbow* – but had failed. Six hundred circulars announcing the venture had elicited only thirty replies. By 1928, by which time he was relatively successful, he again found himself in need of an alternative. His bowdlerised version of *Lady Chatterley's Lover*, retitled (apparently innocuously) as *John Thomas and Lady Jane*, was turned down as too near the mark by both Secker and Knopf. In its unadulterated form, the manuscript had already been complained of as 'distasteful' by his secretary, who had refused to finish typing it, and the job had to be completed by friends.

Surrounded on all sides by doubters, Lawrence embarked on the task of publishing the work himself. He chose a monoglot Florentine, Pino Orioli, to print it and ordered 1,000 copies. Once type had begun to be set, conscience demanded that he should explain to Orioli just what it was he was producing. The printer was unperturbed, remarking

9

only, 'O! Ma! But we do it everyday.' Lawrence promoted the book via small order forms sent to friends, literary agents and booksellers. It would have sold out immediately but for its reception in the magazine *John Bull* as 'FAMOUS NOVELIST'S SHAMEFUL BOOK, A Landmark in Evil' – a comment which led to cancellation of orders and a complete banning of the book's entry into the United States. Nevertheless sales went well enough privately for Lawrence to clear his stocks within months and to order a small reprint before the end of the year.

Some writers have become self-publishers because of their interest in printing. Probably the most illustrious was William Blake, whose writing and illustration became inextricable from the craft of printing itself. His beginnings were unremarkable enough. His first book *Poetical Sketches* was published in 1783, financed by his friends. When no publisher could be found for his next, Blake decided to do it himself. His main interest, in any event, was the combination of writing and illustration, which made working with commercial printers both difficult and expensive. Blake needed complete control. To satisfy his particular requirements, he developed a forerunner of the gravure process. With an impervious liquid he wrote and drew on plates made of copper, removing with acid the parts of the surface which were not to print. The system is in common use today when long runs are demanded, such as for mail-order catalogues or Sunday colour supplements. Blake printed at home, recycling imperfect plates whenever new ones were required.

His first book produced in this fashion, *There is No Natural Religion*, appeared in 1788. The process suited the poet's circumstances perfectly. He mixed his own inks, coloured the illustrations by hand and printed on demand. Mrs Blake did the binding. He never made any money nor, in his lifetime, achieved any kind of artistic success. He continued until his death in 1827 to print up copies of his best-known work, *Songs of Innocence*, and later *Songs of Innocence and Experience*, whenever he found a purchaser.

Unlike Blake, who needed to combine print and text in order to get his message across, William Morris was more interested in the finely made book as an end in itself. He founded his Kelmscott Press in 1890, creating his own founts of type and printing on handmade paper. His methods of design came from the Art and Crafts movement and led eventually to a complete reassessment of British book printing. Morris was a perfectionist. He produced fifty-three volumes during the short life of the press including a number of his own historical romances, *The Wood Beyond The World* and *The Sundering Flood*, as well as a book of his verse, *Poems by the Way*. The crowning glory of his search for the 'book beautiful' was *The Kelmscott Chaucer*, an achievement unsurpassed in printing ever since.

Other notables in the print-it-yourself field include Horace Walpole, who ran the Strawberry Hill Press from his villa in Twickenham. Walpole printed as a diversion – he was wealthy enough to employ a press-man so didn't have to get his hands dirty. He published numerous works, including his own *The Mysterious Mother*, *Hieroglyphic Tales* and, in 1764, *The Castle Of Otranto* – the book which introduced Britain to the horror and mystery of the gothic novel.

In the early twentieth century, Virginia Woolf and her husband Leonard established their Hogarth Press as a hobby. As a respite from the intensity of creative writing, Virginia's afternoons would be spent typesetting. Their first book, *Two Stories*, one by each of them, was published in 1917. Leonard Woolf remarks in his autobiography, 'I must say, looking at a copy of this curious publication today that the printing is rather creditable for two persons who had taught themselves for a month in a dining-room. The setting, inking, impression are really not bad. What is quite wrong is the backing, for I had not yet realised that a page on one side of the sheet must be printed so that it falls exactly on the back of the page on the other side of the sheet.' Despite such shortcomings, the book was a sell-out. The Press went on to become a commercial concern and as an imprint is still publishing today.

The story of Anaïs Nin's printing press is of particular interest. In the 1940s she was already a published novelist. As sometimes happens with writers on the way up, her new novel, *Winter of Artifice*, along with a collection of short stories, *Under a Glass Bell*, was rejected by her American publishers as uncommercial. Nin was more than put out. *Winter of Artifice* had already been published by Obelisk in France and had gained praise from Rebecca West, Henry Miller and Lawrence Durrell among others. Convinced that the publishers didn't know what they were doing, Nin decided to print the book herself.

With the financial assistance of France Steloff of the Gotham Book Mart, who loaned her $100, she purchased a second-hand letter-press and set to work. The books were printed in editions of 300 and distributed *underground*, although Nin remarks 'we did not use the word then'. The break came when, through contacts, the book was favourably reviewed in *The New Yorker*. This resulted in a reprint and, after a long battle, her eventual reacceptance by the commercial world. She says that rather than 'feeling embittered by the opposition of publishers, I was happy they opposed me.' Owning and operating a printing press taught her independence and confidence.

11

She was in direct contact with her public in a way that was otherwise impossible.

Nin's approach is probably the most commonly understood today. Because no one else would publish her, she did so herself.

In 1759, Laurence Sterne had his *Life and Opinions of Tristram Shandy* rejected by the usually faultless publisher Robert Dodsley. Sterne had wanted only the modest fee of £50 for the book's copyright and when turned down decided to publish it as a partwork himself. With the help of a loan he got as far as a highly successful second volume before Dodsley changed his mind and caught up with him. This time Sterne asked for £650 and got it. His career as an author was established for life.

Ezra Pound provides the classic model for unrecognised poets. As a young man in Venice during 1907, he realised that 'a poet with a book of poems to his credit would be more likely to attract attention that one without' and arranged to pay A. Antonini, printer and publisher, to bring out a collection. The work was *A Lume Spento*, seventy-two pages long, published in an edition of 100 copies on paper left over from a history of the church. Pound's distribution was mainly freebies – review copies and complimentaries sent to fellow poets. W. B. Yeats got one, as did both William Carlos Williams and Ella Wheeler Wilcox. He left a few copies with the printer and took what was left with him to London where he sold a number around the bookshops in order to raise the price of his rent.

His burning desire was favourable critical comment of the sort which would precipitate further success. Pound wrote home, 'The American reprint has got to be worked by kicking up such a hell of a row with genuine and faked reviews that Scribner or somebody can be brought to see the sense of making a reprint. I shall write a few myself and get someone to sign 'em.' There was no need. *The Evening Standard* said, 'The unseizable magic of poetry is in this queer paper volume, and words are no good in describing it.' Pound the poet was launched.

All his life he involved himself in the publishing process – starting magazines, persuading publishers to take writers on. He was instrumental in getting Harriet Shaw Weaver of the *Egoist Magazine* to publish Eliot's first book, *Prufrock and Other Observations*, in 1917, even putting up the cash himself. Ezra Pound provides a good example to self-publishers of what can be done through simple determination. Self-published books make excellent stepping stones. If you put yourself behind them they can get you further than you think.

3

THE PRESENT SCENE

Self-publishers of the past would have a lot of trouble recognising the book world of today – we have made many changes. For Alexander Pope and his eighteenth-century compatriots, books were an erudite, gentlemanly activity; you had to be rich to indulge. A quarto volume would cost the same as a pair of breeches, a simple book of essays would cost a family of six the equivalent of a month's supply of tea, while a copy of Boswell's *Life of Johnson* would take a school usher six weeks' work to obtain, and of course you had to be literate. It is often forgotten that mass literacy and mass book production is of comparatively recent arrival. In the eighteenth century, there were fewer people, living shorter lives and only a tiny percentage could read. Even George Bernard Shaw, who a century later took up the publishing of his own plays because he felt he could make more money that way, would find things very different as they are now.

Big business

In Shaw's day, in 1898, the year after Queen Victoria's Diamond Jubilee and the apogee of Empire, there were 99,000 books in print in the UK. A veritable flood; more titles than there were rivers. By the 1990s, pushed by a century of advancing technology and widening education, that figure had risen to over 700,000. New books are now published in Britain at the rate of over 100,000 a year (almost double the figure of ten years ago). A good bookshop is expected to stock a fair range and to have ready access to the rest. Compare that with the seemingly modest 20,000 lines carried by a Tesco superstore. Try going in there to order a particular can of beans they don't happen to have on the shelf.

At any given time, there are around 28,000 firms, individuals and societies who can be regarded as being engaged in publishing of some sort. Of these, only around 3,000 are of interest to booksellers with less than 350 actually commercially publishing books as their main function. When examined, over 60 per cent of the UK turnover in books turns out to be in the hands of under 50 companies. Few of these are truly independent and most form part of one of a very small number of huge conglomerates. Most of the UK publishing names we all recognise – Penguin, Pan, Corgi, Arrow, etc. – are imprints owned by these groups. Who then are all the other firms, the 25,000 out on the fringes? Specialists, learned societies, associations, government departments, quangos, local and regional authorities, pressure groups, and a large number of individuals. Self-publishing is not an uncommon activity.

It was once felt that free libraries would kill the habit of book-buying and that the public would be satisfied with borrowing; they would not wish to own. Yet despite loans in the region of 500 million books a year, down on a decade ago but still pretty hefty a figure, sales continue to rise. TV has not killed the habit, nor computers. There are now over 36,000 shops in the UK engaged in bookselling, although only 3,000 could be said to be proper bookshops. Many are chains: Menzies, Hammicks, Waterstone's, Blackwell's, Dillons, W. H. Smith, Ottakars and Books Etc. A number, if you trace their pedigrees, turn out to have connections with publishers.

Progress, for the book trade is a thrusting industry, is in the area of what are called non-books – over-illustrated tomes with apparently no authors and no editors and nothing indicating who was responsible except the publisher's name; and best-sellers – well-promoted, well-packaged pieces of formula-written hype. The bookshops glitter, but it is all surface. Like goods on show at a petrol station cash-desk, these are all front-out, impulse items. Research has shown that this is the way most people purchase books. They browse and if they see something they like, prettily packaged, they buy. Witness the mass-market paperbacks among the cans at supermarkets. Actual content is secondary, it is all product now.

This is the book world you will be faced with. It sounds huge, frightening and incestuous. But if you follow the advice in this book you'll find a way in.

The alternatives

Keith Smith, doyen of small-publisher marketing, has identified what he calls 'an alternative infra-structure' to the accepted big business norm. Small and self-publishers needn't ape the corporation in order to succeed. It is difficult to generalise but the following broad headings should cover most of what goes on.

Small presses

For the most part literary ventures publishing chapbooks, pamphlets and broadsheets of poetry, avant-garde experimentings, new age philosophy, comic art and the occasional piece of (often dark) fiction. Small presses are a direct product of the increasing accessibility and cheapness of post-war printing technology. They are run by groups of enthusiasts or obsessive individuals, for small-press publishing is no casual hobby. They are started not because anyone has spotted a gap in the market and wants to fill it but because either it is felt that this is the only way to get a vital piece of literature into print, or more commonly because writers who are not published would prefer that they were. Typical contemporary examples are Damnation Publications, Slow Dancer, Sui Generis Publishing and The Lymes Press.

Subsidy publishers and vanity presses

More prevalent in the United States where for many years Edward Uhlan's Exposition was a market leader, although the UK now has its own group of rivals. Strictly speaking subsidy houses rely on the author to contribute towards the cost of printing and origination or to guarantee sufficient sales in order to reduce the publisher's risk to manageable proportions. This would be nothing if not traditional were the publishers concerned large and long-lived but they are not. The precise dividing line between subsidy and vanity is pretty hazy. Both operators are often concerned with the same kind of literary material, both have a shortage of capital along with tiny premises and neither have much clout (and in some cases interest) in the traditional book market.

Subsidy publishers run from the absolutely genuine, publishing for altruistic reasons (many true small presses operate like this), to the tackily dubious who, although carrying out a service, make sure the author pays, and pays well. The common factor uniting all such operations is their universal refusal to declare openly that this is how they work. It is as if public knowledge of any author's money bound up in a publishing venture brings the project into disrepute. Publishers publish, and authors write, so the world believes. Writers accepting the principle of subsidy publishing are advised to take care. Check the charges. Will you get what you are paying for? Is it worth it? It is often far more satisfying and considerably less expensive to do the complete thing alone.

Full-scale vanity presses go a few stages further and should be avoided at all costs. These companies advertise for manuscripts in the classified columns of periodicals, in many magazines aimed at helping writers and in the Sunday newspapers. The usual line is to suggest that fiction, poetry, memoirs and slices of family history are a specialism although they are careful to say that they are also interested in essays, textbooks, literary studies and, in fact, anything they can print. Scripts submitted are unfailingly praised in the highest terms no matter what their quality. They are accepted for publication as a matter of course and usually result in the author being sent a publishing contract of surprising complexity. The first catch lies in the small print. The author must pay 'to help defray the unduly high printing costs at this time' and this is no modest subsidy either. A substantial sum is requested, inevitably way beyond actual market costs, and invariably up-front.

The argument runs, if you can switch yourself away from the blind joy of acceptance long enough to follow it, that this is an investment – in yourself no less – and that the money, along with a fine profit, will all come back to you in your royalties from sales. What they don't tell you is that either all those sales have to be made by you personally, with no help at all from them and at a price too high for the market, or that of the 500 print run mentioned only fifty copies will actually be bound. When you fuss a year later and demand to know what has happened to your unsold books, they either send you the flat sheets or explain that warehouse procedure allows them to pulp non-moving lines. It is in the contract, cloaked in jargon.

Vanity presses make great claims to distribute their titles through the book trade and to send review copies out to the media. It always sounds impressive: copies to the British Library and the *Daily Mirror*. But the trade knows the vanity presses and their books are never reviewed, never stocked, never borrowed. The only people who ever buy vanity press products are the authors themselves.

In recent time the tireless Johnathon Clifford has run an unstinting campaign against what he sees as the creeping evil of unscrupulous vanity operators. Faked-up submissions of appalling quality have been submitted to target presses where they have been universally praised and accepted. This is the vanity press problem – no judgements of quality are ever made. Clifford's evidence of accommodation address dealing, author rip-off and other dubious misdeeds are chronicled in his many campaign reports including *Vanity Press and the Proper Poetry Publisher*, *Vanity Publishers – Marketing, the Facts and the Figures* and *Veiled but Still Vanity*. These are all self-published and available from their author at 27 Mill Road, Fareham, Hants PO16 0TH. In addition Clifford offers a phone, fax and letter advice service to anyone who thinks they have been caught or might be in the process of getting into that state. If anyone in the UK has his finger on this particular pulse it is Clifford. Contact him on 01329 822218. His *Vanity Publishers – the Psychology of Misinformation*, a free hand-out, is a good place to start.

Private presses

The antithesis of vanity publishing, private presses are run for the joy of printing. The quality of the type, the paper and the impression are of utmost importance: the medium is the message. The art of fine and beautiful production must first be satisfied. The quality of the text published is secondary to that.

> A private press may be defined as the typographic expression of a personal ideal, conceived in freedom and maintained in independence.
>
> Will Ransom, *Private Presses and Their Books*

Editions are always small, prices correspondingly high. Distribution is as clandestine as production. The products, if you can get them, are a joy to behold. Typical examples include the Cuckoo Hill Press, the Kit-Cat Press, the Plough Press and the Old Style Press.

The independent publisher

An individual or a partnership who, unlike any of the aforementioned categories, brings out books with profit in mind. Philip and Audrey Ward spent five pages of their excellent manual *The Small Publisher* (Oleander Press) trying to describe the small, independent press and ended up admitting that 'no generalisation is possible'. Independents spring from literary small presses with big ideas, from individuals with a new concept, from partnerships who can see a gap in the market and determine to find and publish the right book to fill it. The vast fringes of conglomerate publishing are shot through with independents – all working eighty-hour weeks and enjoying every minute. Typical examples are Copper Beech Publishing in East Grinstead, John Jones in Ruthin, Bob Lavender's local interest Minimax Books Ltd, the railway publisher Silver Link and some of the many individuals described in Chapter Four.

The non-publisher

An individual, group, society or organisation whose main interest is not publishing but who nonetheless finds it desirable to bring out a book. This is probably the largest and certainly the most amorphous of fringe categories. It includes campaigning groups who ring out propaganda, learned societies who publish transactions, mother-and-baby groups who print guides to infant care, political parties with a policy to expound, voluntary societies raising money, naturalist groups publishing guides to badger trails and multinationals with a corporate profile to bring out. Non-publishers are about as disparate a group as you can get. They are linked by their huge enthusiasms and by a common ignorance of marketing and distribution. Most of them regard it as an affront when the bookseller politely requests a discount.

Shall we proceed? Jonathan Preece of Village Publishing in Monmouth, a community publishing workshop successfully founded on government grant, has this to say:

> We often get writers (usually of autobiography) coming in and asking how much it will cost to have, say, twenty copies of their 200-page book done. It's desperately important for authors to understand the mechanics of printing – what is involved in layout, plate-making, more than one colour ink, etc., in order to have an idea of the costs. They must also understand the difficulty publishers will have in trying to sell books on appallingly narrow subjects to W. H. Smith. I have to say that despite publications like the *Writers' & Artists' Yearbook*, amateurism is rife.

Yet with a bit of knowledge and application self-publishing can be both satisfying and highly successful. Read on.

4

IT CAN BE DONE – PRESENT-DAY SUCCESSES

There have been some great self-published successes in recent times. Hardly a month passes without one or other of the newspapers reporting the tale of unknown authors who get turned down by all the main publishing houses, do the book themselves, only to be rewarded with colossal sales and a Hollywood film deal. Why doesn't everyone do this, muse the reporters? Why indeed?

Most published writers have had difficult starts. Very few have achieved success without a struggle, although the fact that this can happen makes the book world seem at times like the Klondike Gold Rush. A lucky few make it, although most, especially those concerned with fiction or poetry, face rejection at the start of their careers.

The poet and Nobel nominee, R. S. Thomas, was obliged to pay for the Druid Press to bring out his first book and had to help the Montgomeryshire Press with the distribution of *An Acre of Land*, his second. He recalls a curt note being returned with copies he'd hopefully sent to a local bookseller. It read, 'There is no call for work like this in Shrewsbury.' A situation today that could not be further from the truth.

Many writers, especially poets, continue throughout their writing lives to help their publishers. They show up at readings with suitcases of stock. They check bookshops and offer reminders when titles are low. Best-selling poet Dannie Abse can usually be relied upon to produce a copy of almost anything of his, whether it is in print or not. There is nothing wrong with commercial distribution but, as Abse proves, you always sell more if you get involved yourself. The rare Abse titles are those he hasn't actually signed.

For some, however, rejection seems both endless and ultimate. Inability to place work commercially, for any one of a hundred different reasons, is the usual starting point for authors who decide to go it alone.

In the late eighties, running on the coat-tails of Richard Adams's enormous seller *Watership Down*, a west Wales Great Dane breeder, the late Aeron Clement, was having trouble placing his badger novel *The Cold Moons*. Hampered by both lack of dialogue in the book and track record as an author Clement was failing at every turn. He decided reluctantly that there was only one real option open. With the financial help of a local Llandeilo publican he hired a publicist and published the book himself. Reaction was immediate. The new Kindredson Publishing could hardly keep pace with demand. Eventually, knowing well how to spot a winner, Penguin bought the paperback rights and took the book to all those places Kindredson couldn't manage. Self-publishing primed the pump, commerce did the rest. The work is now an established classic.

For decades, Polish émigré Stephan Themerson ran Gaberbocchus Press from Formosa Street in west London. His interest in surrealism and the European avant-garde found fulfilment in a list which included Raymond Queneau, Kurt Schwitters and Raoul Housmann. Themerson also published himself, bringing out titles such as *Cardinal Polatuo*, *The Adventures of Peddy Botton*, and *Wooff, Wooff, or Who Killed Richard Wagner?* to critical, if not quite commercial acclaim. In 1986, by which date Gaberbocchus (the word is Latin for 'jabberwocky') had given up England and moved abroad, Faber & Faber discovered Themerson and published a trade edition of his novel *Mystery of the Sardine*. Success at last and in a way this late acceptance was no bad thing. If he had achieved a mass market earlier, his idiosyncratic and innovative writing would no doubt have become subject to commercial pressures. He would have written differently. Gaberbocchus Press may indeed never have been. Themerson died in 1988.

Going hard for the mass market on his own and actually achieving it is thriller writer Roger Radford. His self-published *The Winds of Kedem*, which came out in 1992, attracted the interest of W. H. Smith, a key outlet for those who sell alone. With them behind it Radford shifted more than 10,000 copies and actually turned a profit. His follow up, *Schrieber's Secrets*, cost him £4,000 which he regards as a good investment. Press interest, Sky TV coverage and further Smith's support will ensure the cash comes back. Radford's Parados Books run on strictly commercial lines.

Artist David Barton is not concerned with the mass market. He knows that interest will be slight. His books consist entirely of drawings – sequences representing a personal philosophy which he finds impossible to convey in words. He works as a part-time teacher with the sole aim of earning enough to finance his publishing. His books range from sixteen-page pamphlets to 336-page perfect-bound paperbacks. At least seventy titles have appeared over the past fifteen years. All come out in editions of 500 with only a handful sold each time; most copies are given away. Barton's work is distinguished, he has exhibited at the Royal Academy and publication in book form is its final realisation. The only way of getting this done successfully is to do it himself.

Autobiography is not the easiest thing to sell unless, of course, you have led a particularly interesting and exciting life. Helga Gerhardi's retelling of her time in Hitler's Germany and as a refugee fleeing into the violent arms of the Russian Army, *Helga*, was rejected by the usual outlets despite numerous authorial slicings to make it shorter. After employing a professional editor to get the standard up and still having the work come back Gerhardi and her family decided to go out alone. With a son able to set the text on computer and a grandson adept at producing advertising flyers as well as handling the distribution the book was a true joint effort. *Helga* appeared under the Virona Publishing imprint in late 1993 and went almost immediately into a second edition. 'We suffered a few delays,' reported the author, 'but that was because the people at the printers spent their time reading the book when they should have been actually printing it.'

Not all self-publishing ventures succeed; some end in utter disaster. Lionel Fanthorpe who, as a writer of pulp fiction during the 1950s had more science fiction books in print than anyone else, found himself in the 1970s without a publisher. His fantasy of sword and sorcery, *The Black Lion*, interested no one. Undaunted he decided to publish it himself, selling his house to raise the funds. Reasoning that this science fiction title should look like all other science fiction titles and should sell in similar numbers, he published what he thought to be an appropriate quantity – 20,000 – all in standard mass-market paperback format. So far so good. It was when he tried to market the book that his troubles began.

Despite constant local publicity, turnover was slow. Fanthorpe and his wife, both natural extroverts, were photographed for the paper dressed as characters from the book. He made appearances on local radio and a full circuit of lectures and talks to local societies. Fanthorpe even ran a science fiction convention in the hope that sales would increase. To little avail; he sold fewer than 6,000 copies. 'In all our innocence,' he comments, 'we really thought that if you wrote a good novel and had it printed, booksellers would be glad to stock it. They weren't. It's all hype, and worry about the cover – the story and the quality of the writing seemed almost irrelevant to the marketing process!!'

Fanthorpe's mistake was to over-reach himself. The market he could tap was 6,000 copies, twelve times David Barton's, but he'd bogged himself down by overprinting. Fifteen years later he has just about recovered.

A lot of writers self-publish because that seems the most appropriate way. Bob Cobbing and Ian Hamilton Finlay are both interested in the non-conventional use of language. At his own Wild Hawthorn Press as well as his son's Morning Star Publications, Finlay works in conjunction with painters, graphic designers, printmakers and other creative partners to produce concrete and post-concrete poetry on cards and in tiny booklets. Bob Cobbing, who is primarily a sound poet and performer, is more interested in the creative possibilities of the printing process itself. His Writers' Forum produces everything from single sheets to fully bound books. Neither artist could consider commercial publication as an option; they both require intimate daily contact with their publications and the only way they can achieve this is by publishing themselves.

Control of his own work allied with the view that there ought to be better ways of making money than simply relying on the royalty pushed Timothy Mo into self-publishing. Mo, a leading UK writer who had twice had his works nominated for the Booker Prize, surprised everyone when he chose to do his novel, *Brownout On Breadfruit Boulevard*, himself. Turning down an advance of £125,000 along with editorial advice to cut his opening ('the filthiest first chapter of any book ever published', as the author himself described it) Mo formed Paddleless Press in 1995. Using friends to edit the text and then lay out the pages via DTP (desktop publishing) was, as Mo put it, 'not as much hassle as organising a British sub-aqua club branch dive'. He employed marketing consultants to sell and a distributor to get the book into the shops, and then with a firm idea of how many he could shift negotiated a competitive price for the final print. Co-ordination, he reports, is the key.

Despite uneven reviews and the difficulties presented by having only one title on your list Mo sold enough both to reprint and to get his investment back. 'I did not want to be down there among the bottles and the dead men,' he said. Self-publishing was the best way of staying both sober and alive.

The speed of success can take a few self-publishers by surprise. The most recent being Jill Paton Walsh, known and respected for her children's books but author of adult work as well. Her *Knowledge of Angels*, an adult fable described by Ursula Le Guin as a 'disturbing and beautiful novel of ideas' was rejected by every one of the nineteen companies it was sent to in the UK, including Weidenfeld & Nicolson, publisher of Paton's two previous adult works. American publishers, however, were keener to chance their arms. Unknown to Walsh a copy of the typescript she had sent to a friend ended up at

Houghton Mifflin where editor Peter Davison was enthusiastic enough to publish immediately. This still had no effect on UK publishers, who collectively refused to amend their original rejection. Quite miffed, Walsh and her partner John Rowe Townsend imported 1,000 copies of a Houghton Mifflin run-on and re-badged them as Green Bay Publications. The book sold so well that Walsh, along with some friends who were willing to put cash into the project, set up Colt Books, employed a professional publicist and took the UK market by storm. Within months the work was shortlisted for the Booker and the paperback rights sold on to Transworld.

Walsh is convinced of the value of professional help. *Knowledge of Angels* had been through the process of both acceptance and careful grooming. 'It was not something that only I thought was good and had not had the professional attention of an editor.' Self-publishing, she warns, 'is only for people who know a lot about the special interests they are addressing; who cannot find a commercial publisher, and who can, if necessary, afford to lose every penny they adventure.'

Erudition in a specialist area led Dr Raymond Turley, a divisional librarian at the University of Southampton, to publish his *Directory of Hampshire and Isle of Wight Art*, a listing of subjects seen at major London art exhibitions between 1760 and 1900. The book was compiled after Turley mistakenly received eight volumes of the *Directory of Royal Academy Exhibitors* on inter-library loan. 'Mindful of the expense,' he remarks, 'I decided not to "waste" what had been supplied.' When completed, the work was offered to the local history society who agreed to publish but only if grant aid could be found. Despite a long search, none was forthcoming. One possible sponsor suggested that if the author cared to add a section detailing the present whereabouts of all art works to which reference had been made, an application would be considered. From Turley's point of view and without the aid of an art world Sherlock Holmes, an impossible task.

This avenue blocked, Turley turned elsewhere. He approached the university, who were already receiving royalties on some of his earlier works. Would they produce the new book directly from his typescript in their print shop? They would. As near as you can get to self-publishing without actually doing it yourself. In academic circles, low print runs for students needing printed dissertations are commonplace and Turley's request for an initial 100 copies was easily met. The book is now in its third reprint, a pleasant surprise for its compiler, and a copy has already been reported stolen from the Isle of Wight County Library – always a good sign of continuing demand.

Self-publisher Jacquelyn Luben's authorial success was actually prompted by tragedy. *The Fruit of the Tree*, her intensely moving auto-biographical account of cot death and miscarriage, reached the UK book market only after its author had singularly failed to sell copies to charter bookshops by leafleting them. Accepting some good, practical advice Luben swallowed her fear of cold calling and tackled her local shops head on. Instead of disappointment she came away with orders and, excited by the prospect of more, began telephoning branches of Waterstone's, nearly all of which ended up taking copies. Persistence got Luben right through a first edition and into a second, all expertly produced, I am assured, at reasonable cost by Ann Kritzinger's short-run print company (see Chapter Thirteen).

Luben's steady biting away at the UK book chains threw up a number of discoveries concerning shops' knowledge of their own stock. When telephoned to see if they would like to reorder some stores declared more copies on the shelves than Luben had originally supplied. Others who the author had never dealt with at all rang her to request permission to return unsolds. Do these places swap stock behind the scenes, asks Luben? It does sound like it, although computer miskeying and sloppy stock checks are a more likely cause.

The Fruit of the Tree has since been reviewed in *Best* as a book of the week and covered by the Open University newspaper, which got the title into a number of OU stockists. Nearly all the national chains carry it. Luben's choice of Nelson Houtman, an authoritative name for her imprint, helped, as did the professional look of the book itself. The thorough approach pays off.

The idea that there might be money somewhere at the bottom of one's particular interest has turned quite a few writers into self-publishers. John Dawes, an expert in swimming-pool technology, regards his subject's innate difficulties as an advantage. Books such as *Swimming Pool Industry Directory and Specifier for Britain and Ireland* and *Introducing Swimming Pool Gardens* have little appeal to the general publisher who would simply be unable to market them. Dawes, however, knows exactly who and where his clients are. His books sell. His particular interest in self-publishing, perhaps fired by an insistence that the hardest part – distribution – be conquered, has led him to form the A–PE, the Author–Publisher Enterprise (see Appendix One).

Journalist Terry Palmer thought there might be a buck or two in local knowledge and set out to cover Constable's country with a guidebook called *The Lower Stour*. What he hadn't counted on was inexperience. In addition to miscalculating the required trade discount, he got his timing wrong. Caught up in the onward rush of production, he found himself taking summer photographs in winter, retouching grey skies blue and often sweeping away snow in order to get a more convincing shot. Ensuing delivery problems resulted in stock arriving at the end of the season rather than the beginning – an unenviable situation as there were no visitors around to buy the books.

Disaster hung at Palmer's shoulders but he persevered. Where most proto-publishers would have given up Palmer gritted his teeth and carried on. Today, twenty years later, he has got publishing beat. He has his own production equipment and is working on gaps in the guide market much further afield. His Heritage House imprint has titles covering everywhere from Morocco to Cyprus and Tunisia to the Gambia. Ventures with fellow travellers have enabled him to encompass the Dominican Republic and Malta as well as an intriguing investigation of ghosts. As a self-publisher Palmer is an example to us all.

Roger Jones runs Ex-Libris Press with his wife from their bookshop in Bradford-on-Avon. His interest in walking has resulted in an attractive list covering both the routes and the philosophy. He has edited *The Walker's Companion*, a selection of footpath writing drawn from the breadth of English literature, and produced a number of local Wiltshire and Devon rambler's guides. His great work, however, is *Green Roads to Land's End*, a marvellous travelogue which describes a foot-blistering hike from London to Cornwall complete with maps, drawings and blow-by-blow accounts of the effects differing terrains have on damaged feet.

Jones began publishing while still working as a librarian. He'd completed a town history and, although inexperienced in printing, gambled that his knowledge of local reading habits would see him through. It did. Market familiarity is at least half of publishing – he sold 1,000 copies of his first title in three weeks.

Self-publishing can win rewards where commercial publishing flounders. Philip Ward has tried both and prefers the former for just this reason. He is a travel writer, dramatist, poet, historian and founded the Oleander Press with his wife Audrey while, like Roger Jones, still working as a librarian. Although never intended as a major outlet for his own writings – Ward has been happily published by Faber and others – this is what it became. Books which could easily have found commercial publishers became Oleander's. These included the long series of guides Ward prepared to North Africa, Indonesia, the Middle East, Japan, three books on Bulgaria and four detailed regional guides to India. His *Contemporary Designer Bookbinders* is a major illustrated reference book, unique in its field. The 768-page *Ha'il: Oasis*

City of Arabia could have proved a problem but Ward makes a virtue of surmounting difficulties.

He admits only one case, his *Oxford Companion to Spanish Literature*, where the publisher's imprint was able to generate more sales than his own. Generally, the Oleander Press is best. His amazing *A Lifetime's Reading* has run to more than 10,000 copies while *The Small Publisher* has reached nearly 2,000. Not at all bad for a hardback costing nearly £15.

Self-publishing is an individual affair which collectively amounts to a vast enterprise. There are thousands participating. If they can do it, why not you?

5

HOW TO SET YOURSELF UP

Thus begins the innocently arrogant, thoroughly pleasant process
of self publication.

Robin Chapman

At the outset you simply get up one morning and say you are going
to do it. There are no registrations, no forms to fill in and no associations that you must join. But you will need capital. Even at its most
inexpensive, self-publishing requires some input of cash. Luckily this
is not like film-making where to get through the door costs an arm
and every step of the way uses up a leg. Self-publishing, of a sort, is
available to the individual with four reams of paper at a few pounds
a time and free access to a photocopier. However, for anything worthy
of being called a book you need to think in terms of at least a couple
of thousand pounds. Volumes such as *How to Publish Yourself*, with
its professional design and editing, can cost considerably more.

To be more specific over costs is difficult; there are so many variables – origination, paper, process, extent. You can make a book cost
almost anything. Self-publishing is easily affordable by those earning
an income, but also manageable by the retired and by those on support.

It is perhaps best in the beginning not to bank on getting your
money back. Publishing is a profession of uncertainty. If you calcu-
late prices correctly and make no marketing blunders then you might
sell all you produce – there may be a small profit, if you've arranged
things that way and this is a bonus. Most self-publishers operate
somewhere between a hint of profitability and total loss – but not all.
As you will have seen from Chapter Four, some have produced best-
sellers, and some have gone on to establish commercial businesses
with the returns from their early success. It all depends on your aims.

In the commercial field, it is reckoned that out of every ten books
published three lose money, four break even and three go into profit.
Blockbusters are rare. The dreadful flop occurs every day. Large
publishers can work on an average; the self-publisher has only one
chance.

Publishing can only be made to pay if you don't value your own
time at all.

Jonathan Cape

27

If you have got a job then do not give it up to become a self-publisher. Publish in your spare time until you can see where you are.

Where to raise the cash

Banks

Self-publishing as commercial enterprise rather than paying hobby is the stance to adopt when approaching a bank. Loans may be offered, but take them on with care. Profits from publishing can be a notoriously long time materialising. It has been argued that the process is such an intricate and detailed affair that eventual sales hardly justify the expenses involved. This may be true of many projects but not all. Good profits are there if you have the ideas and the experience. Self-publishers though, are unlikely to find their titles racked out with the sausages at Sainsbury's and would in any event find the simple act of national distribution from garage or bedroom difficult to manage. Self-publishing is small publishing: there is a limit to what one person can do.

If you do intend operating commercially, be sure that you can do it all on your own. Present the bank with a detailed business plan – what and why you are publishing, your costings, your marketing plans and your imagined outcome. You will need to believe wholeheartedly in your project's success. Be prepared to put in immensely long hours. This is business we are talking about here. But then, if you enjoy it, it is not quite like work.

Arts boards

If your venture is less a business and more an act of creative-writing – self-publishing as described in Chapter Two – then one would imagine it easy enough to obtain a grant from one of the many local arts boards, councils and associations. Unfortunately this is almost uniformly not the case. It is not that creative writing and small publishing themselves are ineligible for aid. They are not. It is the self-publishing that apparently disqualifies. A number of boards regard as suspect individuals sponsoring their own books and most will only consider aid if the publisher and author are unconnected. The fear of subsidising vanity rather than art is real. Despite this, arts boards are often able to advise on local printing co-operatives, marketing initiatives, subsidised promotion schemes and the like. Coverage varies from region to region with some far more interested in the fate of literary ventures than others.

28

All associations run a magazine or news-sheet of some sort. These range from a photocopied handout of information for writers' circles to professionally produced glossies containing articles and reviews. Such periodicals will almost certainly be willing to give coverage to local creative activities.

As an alternative the notion of self-publishing could be dropped and, with an accomplice, a genuine small press established. Plan to publish more than one title. Such ventures *are* eligible for grant aid in some regions. Take care to avoid out-and-out deception.

The arts board for your area should be in the telephone directory. If in doubt consult the listings in either A. & C. Black's annual *Writers' & Artists' Yearbook* or Macmillan's *The Writer's Handbook*, edited by Barry Turner.

Arts Councils

A step-up from the boards, these are even less likely to sponsor a self-published title, although they do run a number of promotional and other initiatives and are usually a good point of contact for information and advice. There are four in the UK – England, Wales, Scotland and Northern Ireland as well as a southern Irish council in Dublin. Contact details can be found in the yearbooks referred to above.

Lottery and pools money

Applications to the National Lottery are a possibility, although for a self-publisher meeting the criteria may be difficult. The sums of money asked for can be large. Contact the Lottery c/o your national Arts Council. The Foundation for Sport and the Arts, which distributes pools money, has a similarly complex set of application criteria. Terms and conditions, however, are regularly amended so it is always worth asking. The Foundation for Sport and the Arts is at PO Box 20, Liverpool L13 1HB (0151 259 5505).

Sponsorship

Current economic thinking favours free enterprise helping the arts to help themselves. Sponsorship is available from big business to those activities which by association are most likely to enhance a company's identity. An oil company will benefit by having its name in an opera programme; a wine wholesaler will promote piano recitals because the image is right. For the business there can be tax savings too. Such considerations are unlikely to be of use to the self-publisher but sponsorship at a lower level need not be completely ruled out. A brewery may consider sponsoring a sports book, small businesses may help your guide to local eating, while on a different scale the council may wish to be associated with a history of the town.

The late Mogg Williams, a former miner and a folk poet of the south Wales coalfields, very successfully financed his collection of verse *Mogg's People* by selling advertising space in it to local shops. His previous books, all self-published, which commented stringently on the lot of the miner in the 1980s amid closing pits and devastated communities, were sponsored by the National Union of Miners and during the long strike by various miners' support groups.

The Association for Business Sponsorship of the Arts (ABSA), an independent membership organisation set up by and for businesses who wish to sponsor the arts publishes a useful handbook. *The ABSA/W. H. Smith Sponsorship Manual* is available at a small charge. Contact ABSA at Nutmeg House, 60 Gainsford Street, Butlers Wharf, London SE1 2NY (0171 378 8143).

To gain sponsorship you will need to write a lot of letters. Stress the benefits to the community in what you are doing. There is no gain for a business sponsor simply to be associated with vanity. Pick companies with a large public. Concentrate your efforts on those with a previous record of sponsorship or those who would gain the most from being connected with what you are trying to do.

Other sources

If you are willing to hunt a little there are a number of other sources of help available. The UK is well served with a network of TECs – Trading and Enterprise Councils, (known as LECs – Local Enterprise Councils – in Scotland), Local Enterprise Agencies and other local and centrally funded advice centres. Ring Business Link (0345 567765) in England and Scotland or Business Connect (0345 969798) in Wales who will put you in touch with your nearest appropriate contact.

Enterprise agencies are funded from a mix of local authority, government and private sources. Their brief is to support new ventures and, so long as you are willing to angle it appropriately, self-publishing can be made to count. The key here is to be seen to be establishing yourself not as a writer but as a publisher. The fact that your first title will be by yourself is incidental. The agencies will see you as a potential future employer or at very least as an enterprise viable enough to keep you off the streets for a bit. They will offer you training in marketing and production, help you formulate a business plan, identify your funding short-fall and put you in touch with all available sources of finance from local authority grant aid to bank loans.

Start-up help under the New Business programme which offers assistance in the form of a small weekly grant running for six months may be just what you need. On the other hand if you are still young (twenty-nine years old appears to be the official watershed) then assistance from the Prince's Youth Business Trust may be applicable. Or your local authority may run a community development programme which you can access. Much depends on where you live. The maze of possibilities may be complex but enterprise agencies know all the angles. If your publishing is to be of any scale they can certainly help see you through.

Private loans

The final approach and the most traditional. The private patron goes back to before the birth of print. I have heard of writers advertising in the newspapers for them but I have no knowledge of how successful such a ploy may be. If you have connections use them. If you haven't, you can always ask your family and friends. Spread the burden widely. If the project fails, small amounts may be forgotten; large debts stay in memory for a considerable time.

Technicalities

Business names

All self-publishers are advised to adopt a name other than their own under which to trade. This is the publishing *imprint* and its existence will add credibility to the venture. Disc jockey Ron Ellis is convinced that he sold far more copies of his self-done Cape-poetry-lookalike *Diary of a Discotheque* under the Nirvana Books imprint than he would have under his own name. The list of Nirvana Books consisted entirely of one title, but only Ron Ellis knew that. Adopt an air of enterprise, give the impression that there are more than one of you. If you succeed that may well turn out to be the case.

The name chosen should unite commercial usefulness with authorial aims. Nirvana Books suited Ellis perfectly by combining a reference to publishing with that of an artistically stimulating mental state. Had the imprint been called, for example, 'Heavenly Enterprises', then the image presented would have been completely wrong.

There are few restrictions on the name you choose and no registration is required. It is advisable, though, to avoid selecting a name already in use elsewhere. Check with Companies House, Crown Way,

31

Cardiff CF4 3UZ (01222 388588). There are also a number of sensitive words and expressions which cannot be used as part of a business name without permission. These include 'bank', 'royal', 'foundation' and 'international'. The restriction is to prevent individuals from implying that their business is something that it is not. Again check with Companies House. A set of notes for guidance is available free of charge. Business names used on letters, orders for goods and services, invoices, receipts, etc., must be supplemented by a reference to the name of the actual owner. This can best be accomplished by printing at the foot of the document something like 'Ron Ellis trading as Nirvana Books' or 'Ron Ellis sole proprietor'.

You should inform your bank and open an appropriate account. Payments to you will be made in the name of the business and these are usually ineligible for clearance through your private account.

Copyright

In broad terms a complex subject, but for the purposes of self-publishing relatively simple. The provisions are contained in the Copyright, Designs and Patents Act 1988 and enhanced by the memorably renamed Duration of Copyright and Rights in Performance Regulations 1995. This body of legislation provides, among other things, for the protection of the writer's text but not the ideas or the images or the sense of that text. Copyright covers the actual form and style of words used, rather than what they say. It applies to completed books, fragments, notes, even the preliminary written sketch you may make on the back of an envelope. Copyright covers handwritten, printed and electronic material, be it in single or multiple copies. This protection is yours until you die, when it passes to your estate and then persists for a further seventy years before emerging into the public domain. In addition an author has the right to be identified in print as the originator of a piece of work, no matter who actually ends up owning the copyright. So long as the writer has 'asserted' his or her 'moral rights' by including an appropriate statement to this effect either at the end of the text or with the publication data at the start of the book the rights are secure. A typical assertion might read: 'Peter Finch is hereby identified as author of this work in accordance with Section 77 of the Copyright, Designs and Patents Act 1988.'

There is no registration for copyright under British law. It is yours the moment you cause written words to come into being. Copyright under international law is protected by including on the verso of the title page the symbol © followed by the date and the name of the copyright holder. Thus: © 1998 Peter Finch.

Copyright is like property. It is possible to sell it and to rent it. If you sell it then it will be the purchaser's name which appears next to the copyright symbol rather than your own. If you rent, as in the case of allowing an item of your work to appear in an anthology edited by another, then the copyright in the item itself remains entirely yours. The selection, the run of choices used in that anthology, will be the copyright of the editor.

It was the practice, common before the Copyright Act of 1911, for writers to sell their copyrights outright. With the advance of the royalty system such deals have been largely supplanted.

If you wish to quote from or use sections of the work of others in your book, authorisation is usually required from the copyright holder *in advance* and a fee payable. By convention, British publishers have agreed that in order to get round the problem of the unscrupulous beginning their books 'As Bill Bryson says ...' and then proceeding to quote the whole of *Notes from a Small Island*, quotations shall be limited to a single extract of up to 400 words of prose, or a series of extracts of not more than 300 each and up to a total of 800 words, or forty lines of poetry but not more than a quarter of a poem. The overriding factor is that the quotation must not represent a substantial part of the original work. The system is known as 'fair dealing'. The let-out under the acts is that a certain amount of quotation for the purposes of research, criticism or review is allowed without permission so long as sufficient acknowledgement is given. In all cases a written acknowledgement is required.

In addition to written work, copyright also exists in illustrated material, works of art, maps and photographs. Here it usually rests with the artist or photographer responsible except for commissioned works where it rests with the initiator of the commission. Should you wish to use such copyright material permission must be obtained in advance.

A good outline summary of copyright law appears in Amanda L. Michaels' article in the *Writers' & Artists' Yearbook*. An essay by Barry Turner on the practical implications can be found in *The Writer's Companion*.

Plagiarism

Another illusion, seldom entertained by competent authors is that...others are waiting to plagiarise their work. I think it may be said that the more worthless the manuscript, the greater the fear of plagiarism.

Sir Stanley Unwin, *The Truth About A Publisher*

Plagiarism is much less prevalent than most people think. There are far more ideas, images, poems and stories around than there are places to publish them. Why bother to steal? Although unfounded, it is still a common fear. If your written words are used, without your permission, then you have a right to legal recourse against the user. If your work is found masquerading as the work of others, you have a right to a similar action, although the case will be harder to prove. If you are in real fear of this happening it is possible to take out some insurance and deposit copies at Stationers' Hall who will charge you £35.25 for a registration covering seven years (the Registrar, The Worshipful Company of Stationers and Newspaper Makers, Stationers' Hall, Ave Maria Lane, London EC4M 7DD 0171 248 2934), or more simply send a copy of the typescript to yourself by registered mail and *without opening* it keep it in a safe-deposit at your bank. Such rather extreme precaution will establish beyond doubt the existence of a specific work at a specific date. This is a prerequisite in a successful action for plagiarism and will, no doubt, help some people sleep at night.

Libel

This is defamation published in permanent form. It is unlikely that self-publishers will find themselves in court but in times of changing values the possibility, no matter how remote, is worth guarding against. An action for libel is usually a civil one with the aim of obtaining both damages and a court injunction to prevent repetition. Legal aid is not available. A successful action needs to prove that the libel was published by the defendant (you), refers to the plaintiff (the person libelled) and is defamatory. It is no defence to say that you didn't mean it or that your intentions have been misunderstood. Libel actions can be defended by proving that the statements were justified, or were the truth or fair comment.

Occasionally, criminal prosecutions are made against those responsible for perpetuating a libel. The circumstances usually involve statements regarded as obscene, seditious, blasphemous or inciting racial hatred. Those responsible can include the bookseller and the printer as well as the publisher. Legal advice should always be taken if problems arise.

Book-keeping, tax and VAT

Keeping records of income and expenditure probably seems of minor importance to a self-publisher. Initially, there are few transactions and they are spaced far apart. The problem comes when things start to multiply, as they have a habit of doing, and cheques in payment of invoices and bills for services arrive by every post.

A simple cash book (or spreadsheet program if you are computer literate) is the answer. Date and record all transactions from the outset. Retain your receipts and make copies of all bills. This will enable you to keep track of your finances and to accurately cost the overall venture. Unless you clearly appear to be making money, the tax office shouldn't bother you although under self-assessment you are now obliged to keep records of all you do. Even if you do find yourself in the lucky position of moving from the red side of your bank balance into the black, it does not necessarily mean that tax is payable. Read the sections relevant to taxation for writers in *The Writers' & Artists' Yearbook* and employ an accountant. Their fees will almost certainly be covered by the amount they will help you save.

VAT is not yet levied on books but there are continuing rumours that eventually it will be. It is charged on all supplies and services including those for individual aspects of book production. Complete books remain zero-rated, VAT free. In other words if, as a publisher, you separately employ your own typesetter and binder, the invoices for their services will carry VAT. If the printer employs these firms on your behalf and subsequently provides you with one full invoice for the complete job (for *books*) then it will be VAT free.

Under appropriate circumstances VAT can be recovered by registering a publishing business for VAT purposes but most self-publishers will operate at too low a level to be considered.

International Standard Book Numbers

ISBNs are unique reference numbers printed on a book's back jacket and the verso of its title page. There is no formal obligation on self-publishers to use them, but they will benefit enormously if they do. ISBNs consist of a ten-digit series which identifies the country of origin, the publishers and the specific work. The final digit is a check digit which mathematically checks the correctness of the preceding nine. For example 0 74900 301 4 from this book, where 0 identifies Britain, 74900 Allison & Busby, 301 this specific edition and 4 the check digit. Numbers are allocated, free of charge, by the ISBN Agency, a division of J. Whitaker & Sons Ltd at 12 Dyott Street, London WC1A 1DF (0171 420 6000).

Self-publishers are advised to request an ISBN from the Agency as soon as they have a definite title for their book. Those with a list of titles are encouraged to purchase the print-out of a block of ISBNs and to allocate the numbers themselves.

Down the corridor from the ISBN Agency are Whitaker's Bibliographic Services. This division of the company is able to help publishers considerably by including their titles in a number of bibliographic directories and lists. Publishers are required, at least three months in advance of publication, to complete a Whitaker's *Information form* detailing their work. This enables the title to be included in the weekly booklist published in *The Bookseller*. This periodical, 'the organ of the book trade', is used by both bookseller and librarian as a prime source of reference for new titles. Inclusion in it will inevitably result in sales. Notified titles are entered in Whitaker's main *Bibliographic File*, a comprehensive database of some two million English language titles. This database is used as the source for a variety of information publications in hard-copy, on-line, microfiche and disk versions including *Bookbank*, *Whitaker's Web*, *British Books in Print*, and *New and Forthcoming Books*, as well as a variety of directories covering publishers' names and addresses and ISBNs. The database is used by Teleordering, the book trade's computer-based ordering system, and is also sold on to bibliographic database providers abroad, including the United States. Whitaker's service is absolutely invaluable and, to the self-publisher, entirely free. Fuller details together with a supply of *information forms* can be had by writing to their main office listed above.

Bar codes

These are the machine-readable stripes found on almost all consumer products these days. They represent a thirteen-digit sequence consisting of the prefix 978 representing the product (a book), the first nine digits of your unique ISBN plus a new check digit. Supplementary bar codes known as 'add-ons' can also be obtained to represent the price. In a trade where stock control, ordering, sales data and till operations are increasingly handled by computer, bar codes can be regarded as an essential part of book production. Once you know your ISBN a code can be prepared for you in hard-copy, disk or film format by one of a number of specialist providers. Bar codes should always appear on the book jacket, back, bottom right. Print them as they are – do not reverse them out in order to improve the design, as one small publisher of my acquaintance did. Code readers in shops like things simple. Bar codes for self-publishers can be obtained from Axion Auto ID Ltd, Church Road, Weston-on-the-Green, Bicester OX6 8QP (01869 351155) or Axis Multidata, Maestro House, 4 Fir Road, Bramhall, Stockport SK7 2NP (0161 440 9877).

British Library Cataloguing-in-Publication data programme

This provides for library catalogue information to be supplied to the library service at least three months in advance of publication. This information is included in the British National Bibliography available to libraries and other interested parties worldwide. Participation is not compulsory but is free. It will certainly help sales and is thoroughly recommended. CIP data details the title's Dewey decimal classification, and its Library of Congress subject heading, along with information on its author set out in a format usable by library catalogue systems. Publishers today, other than those in developing countries, have dispensed with actually printing this data in their books substituting instead on the verso of the title page the standard acknowledgement:

British Library Cataloguing-in-Publication Data
A catalogue record for this book is available from the British Library

The scheme is administered for the British Library by BDS (Bibliographic Data Services) Ltd, 24 Nith Place, Dumfries DG1 2PN (01387 266004), who can provide advance information forms. Further details can also be obtained directly from the British Library, National Bibliographic Service, Boston Spa, Wetherby, West Yorkshire LS23 7BQ (01937 546989).

Starting in self-publishing is no more complex than assembling a flat-pack wardrobe from MFI. It can be done on the kitchen table with a pot of glue and some scissors. Work progressively. Learn as much as you can from anyone in the profession of books you come into contact with. As a new self-publisher you are a small and inexperienced operator. You must learn to help yourself.

6

WHAT DOES A BOOK LOOK LIKE

We all imagine we know how it goes – a cover, pages with text on, one at the front saying who the book is by, perhaps a reference in small print somewhere to the printer or is that only with magazines? It might sound obvious, but even if you read and handle books every day you will not be fully conversant with their component parts until you have to make one yourself. I say *make* and not *write*. The two are different. This chapter deals with how to proceed once the inspiration, the drafting and the polishing are at an end.

Begin by finding a model. This should be a published book of similar size to how you imagine your own to be and one which appeals to you in both style and format. This will be something to which you can aspire. Before going any further have a look at your own bookshelves. You should notice a great deal of variety. If you study books as artefacts rather than literature, you'll discover that once beyond the conventions of cover, title page, contents list, text and so on there is apparently no common agreement on the way things should be done. Should your paragraphs begin by being indented – as they do in the present volume? Should there be line spaces between them? Should chapter headings be in the centre of the page or ranged left? Should quotations be isolated, indented and set in smaller type, or should they be absorbed into the body of the text? These questions of detail are the responsibility not of the printer but of the publisher and that's you.

The best place for your model is not the library, where books are often rebound and covered before issue, but the bookshop. This is the marketplace where the latest innovations will be on show. Here are the products of *contemporary* publishing. Here also is the competition you'll face when you enter the field. Take a good look. Study format. You'll find few A4 floppies, no funny shapes and certainly nothing more than a foot and a half wide. For your book, plan on the normal. Become bookseller-acceptable: it's the easiest route.

If you are serious about self-publishing, have a talk to the shop manager or the shop buyer. They have a wealth of experience in dealing with publishers and will be able to advise on the best style and format. While here, find out if they'd buy copies should you produce it. You'll have to do this sooner or later so why not start now. Make these investigations in the morning, never at lunchtime or on

Saturdays. Booksellers are hard to get a sensible answer out of at peak times.

Your chosen model should be as near to how you see your own book looking as you can manage. Avoid the expensive, the obviously flashy and the clearly de luxe.

It is worth mentioning the differences between a book and a pamphlet. For the purposes of Public Lending Right there are none, although this was not always the case. To be classed as a book it needs to be printed and offered for sale, nothing more. UNESCO has a rather tougher specification. For them a book is 'a non-periodical, printed publication of at least forty-nine pages exclusive of cover'. How you end up defining it will really be coloured by how you feel about it. A sixty-page collection of old and embarrassing juvenilia is clearly a pamphlet while thirty-two pages of important new poetry just has to be a book.

Anatomy

If you examine any regularly published book you will find that as well as its main subject matter there will be a number of pages of additional miscellaneous information. These will run prior to the start of the work and in many cases will also follow its end. These pages, known as *preliminary matter* and *end matter* may appear of little significance to the amateur but are actually very important. They constitute the structure within which your text will dwell. In order to appear as professional as possible, your book should follow these conventions. If nothing else they will make it easier both to handle and trace. It is to your advantage to conform.

Not all of the list of items which follows will be necessary in every book. Conventional fiction does not require an index, for example. Indeed many books never get beyond the first six of the fifteen items I've listed. Before proceeding check your models. Have a look at what others have done. Here are two customs worth noting:

● When you open a book, the page on the right-hand side is known as the *recto*; its reverse is the *verso*.

● Page numbering will follow one of two conventions, either: (a) the preliminaries are regarded as part of the book proper and page one is therefore the first page you come to (by far the simplest system) *or:* (b) the preliminaries are numbered with roman numerals (i to xii) and page one is the first page of actual text.

Preliminaries (known as 'prelims')

Page 1. *The half-title* sometimes known as the *bastard-title*. Conventionally this consists of the name of the book in splendid isolation. It is *always* a recto.

Page 2. Often left blank or used to list the author's previous publications, other books in the series or publisher's advertising matter. Occasionally this page is used to present a drawing or photograph of some sort.

Page 3. *The title page.* Should contain the book's full title, any subtitle and the name(s) of the author(s) or editor(s) together with the name of the publisher. This is always a *recto*.

Page 4. *The title-page verso.* Contains all the bibliographic data relating to the book and is the page where error most often creeps in. On page 41 is a typical example, taken from Denis Ratcliffe's tale of wartime Swansea, *Second Chances*. Starting at the top the information found here is as follows:

a) Publisher's name and address. Absolutely vital information for anything published, especially self-published works where your name is less likely to appear in the usual trade directories. It is amazing how many books are published which lack this information and how many sales and readers are lost as a result. The publisher in our example is Seren, an imprint of Poetry Wales Press Ltd. I would recommend that self-publishers also include their post codes and their phone numbers.

b) The copyright line: © followed by your name and the date. This protects the book under international conventions (see Chapter Five).

c) British Library Cataloguing in Publication data acknowledgement (see Chapter Five).

d) ISBN – International Standard Book Number (see Chapter Five).

e) *All rights reserved*, which means that if anyone wants to make a film of your book, quote from it extensively, reproduce it on-line or on CD-ROM, translate it into Bengali or use its storyline to sell crisps, then your permission, as owner of the *rights*, is first required.

f) Acknowledgement of financial assistance towards the book's

40

production, if you've been lucky enough to get any – in this case from the Arts Council of Wales.

g) Details of cover art used, along with appropriate acknowledgement.

h) Details of the printer, along with the actual typeface used. Some publishers go further and include data such as

Set in 11 on 13 pt Sabon by Rowland Photosetting, Bury St Edmunds, and printed on Glastonbury Ivory antique laid paper

But unless your production is really special it is best not to brag.

i) You should also use the verso as the place to assert your moral rights (see Chapter Five).

seren is the book imprint of
Poetry Wales Press Ltd
Wyndham Street, Bridgend
Wales

Contents © Denis Ratcliffe, 1996

A CIP Record for this book is available from
the British Cataloguing in Publication Data Ofice

ISBN 1-85411-151-5

*The publisher acknowledges the financial support of the
Arts Council of Wales*

Cover illustration: 'Bombed house and shop' by Will Evans
reproduced courtesy of the Glynn Vivian Art Gallery:
Swansea City Council Leisure Services Department

Printed in Times by WBC Book Manufacturers, Bridgend

Page 5. Blank or *dedication*. This is not in the least obligatory and can range from the servile and grovelling, such as this example from a Scots author of 1815:

> To the Right Honourable the Earl of Breadalbane. May it please your lordship, with overpowering sentiments of the most profound humility, I prostrate myself at your noble feet, while I offer to your lordship's high consideration these very feeble attempts to describe the indescribable ...

to the simple

For my parents

Laurence Sterne marked the dedication page of his *Tristram Shandy* as 'To be let or sold for fifty guineas' which is a fair idea. If you have been helped, financially or otherwise, in the writing of your book then it can be a nice gesture to dedicate it to your benefactor.

Page 6. Blank.

Page 7. *Contents*. Appropriate if it is a non-fiction work divided into chapters, or for a book of poems or short stories where individual titles need to be located. It is of less significance with novels, although I have come across examples where, rather pointlessly, a series of unnamed chapters are listed by number.

Page 8. Blank.

Page 9. *List of illustrations,* if there are any.

Page 10. Blank.

Page 11. *Foreword*. Traditionally, this is an endorsement of what you've written, often in the form of an introduction made by an authority in your chosen field or a figure from public life. I've always felt forewords to be a total waste of time, rather like testimonials. They can have no possible claim to be objective. If they said the work was bad you wouldn't include it, would you? But if you can squeeze a good one out of someone then there is nothing much lost by putting it in.

Page 12. Blank.

Page 13. *Preface* or *introduction*. Your chance to give your rationale: to explain why you wrote what you did. Prefaces are usually signed or initialled,and give the place where you completed the work and the date. Mine would be 'P.F., Cardiff, 1997'. You can score points by making your place of completion somewhere more exotic.

Page 14. Blank

Page 15. *Acknowledgements*. It often happens (as it did in the case of this book) that a lot of people offer help of some sort or another. It is vitally important, especially to a self-publisher operating on a shoestring, to offer thanks to those who have checked references, offered suggestions, read the text, pointed out errors, word processed the manuscript and made the tea. Put them all in; as many as seems reasonable. Those you can't afford to donate copies to will undoubtedly buy.

Page 16. Blank.

Page 17. The text itself. Chapter One, the first poem. This should *without variance* start on a recto.

End matter

End pages, which follow the main text, should always start on a new leaf. They can include the following:

1 *Appendices and notes*. If needed should follow the text directly, always commencing on a recto.

2 *Lists* – references, bibliographies of other works you may have referred to in the text, recommendations for further reading, etc.

3 *The index*. The complication of this can be the subject of a book in itself (Larry S. Bonura's *Art of Indexing*, Wiley). There are also a number of proprietary word processing programmes which have indexing facilities although using them is no simple matter. A good index is a massive advantage to a factual work. It is a selling point, it lends authority, it makes the book look well dressed. Someone really well attired needs to be in your company for some time before you notice the cut of their clothes. A good index, hiding itself at the end of the volume, will be like that. They are best compiled at page-proof stage (we'll come to proofs later) and are done as a separate operation from proof-reading. If you are doing this without computer aid set yourself up with a pile of 3 x 5 file cards and, as you read through your text, make one out for every significant person, place, event, book title, etc., you come across.

43

In Harry Mulholland's self-published climber's guide *The Irish Munros*, there is an index which lists places ('Bianconi Inn', 'Curraghmore Lake'), items of equipment ('books', 'clothes', 'maps') and then subdivides the larger headings, such as 'Eire' into 'climate', 'highest mountains', 'population', etc. The aim is to answer all reasonable requests for information with a reference. Check a number of contemporary examples to see how it is done. Works of fiction do not have indices. Collections of poetry often substitute an index of first lines, although this is more common with anthologies than it is with first collections.

As I've indicated, not every book will need all these prelims and end pages. In fact, a full apparatus such as I've described would look quite pretentious surrounding eight pages of verse or a brief essay on the history of the local church. Check your bookshelves and in practice you'll find that there are many possible variations, substitutions and omissions. Most average, traditionally designed books, however, will follow form to some degree. The very least you could provide on a slim volume and still get away with would be title page, title-page verso and then the text commencing on a recto. Horrors to be avoided at all costs include the text commencing on a verso, which looks ugly, or a title page on a verso, which makes no sense; and the information normally contained on the title-page verso missing altogether. This happens all too frequently and makes the librarian's, bookseller's and book user's task impossible. Do not, unless it is your avowed aim, be eccentric. The traditional approach will help you sell more books. Check your models. If in doubt, include. If it does nothing else it will give you a bigger book.

7

GETTING IT TOGETHER –
THE PRESENTATION OF COPY

The parts of your book now need to be drawn together for the printer
– prelims, text and end matter – forming what is known as copy.

Even if you intend to carry out some or all production yourself
clearly edited, cleanly presented and durably prepared copy is a prerequisite. The first stage in the production process is have the material
set in type. You may chose to go with whatever comes out of your
word processor (or your typewriter for that matter) and more of this
anon. But for the moment let us consider how you should present your
material to a third party for translation into print-quality type. This
task traditionally fell to a person known as the typesetter and it was
blue-collared, inky fingered work. But all that's gone – the trays of
movable metal type, the wooden chases, even the monstrous hot-metal
Linotype setting machines are now in museums. Today text is invariably set using a desk-top keyboard and arranged on a standard
computer screen. This task is carried about by a reprographic bureau.
The job of the bureau is literally to *copy* what is presented *regard-
less of any mistakes* it may contain. Do not expect your errors to be
corrected, your misspellings put right or your misspacings realigned.
The bureau will not read the sense of what you have presented but
will copy exactly what they find. Prepare with great care.

1   Key your copy, double-spaced, on white A4 paper. One side of
    the page only.
2   Hand corrections and alterations should be made *above* the line.
    Try to keep these to a minimum. If it looks untidy then correct,
    rekey and prepare again.
3   Leave wide margins on both sides and a good space top and
    bottom. This area will be used for printer's or setter's instructions.
4   To avoid ambiguity over the extent of your text give it a catch-
    title. If it were this present book you could call it 'How To'.
    Number each page of textural matter, top right, 'How To 1', 'How
    To 2', and so on. To provide a kind of belt and braces, the word
    'more' can be put at the bottom right of each sheet and, most impor-
    tantly, the word 'ends' at the foot of the final page.
5   If you would like your paragraphs indented, mark the first word
    with a square bracket. If no indent is required, insert a horizontal

line between the first word of the paragraph and the left-hand margin. The misuse of paragraph indents is often the mark of the amateur self-publisher. The initial paragraph of any chapter carries no indent at all. Subsequent paragraphs always do. The indent should be no more than one *em*. This is a typographer's measure, the dimensions of which vary depending on the typeface and point size used. The constituent paragraphs of a section or chapter of a book should be run next to each other and not separated by blank lines.

6   If you are keying your copy on a typewriter the conventions are that words underlined will be set in *italic* type. Words underscored with a wavy line will be set in **bold**.

7   If you are using a word processor you will face no such difficulties. Most programs can alter print from *italic* to **bold** with a single key-stroke. Word-processed hard copy should still be prepared in the style just described. Cost savings, however, may be possible by letting the bureau have access to your original disks. And even if the cash savings here turn out to be minimal you will still save by avoiding errors of transcription. You will need to confer to ensure that the bureau's equipment can read your computer's output. Amstrad PCW 3' Locoscript disks are almost universally unacceptable while standard 3.5' disks of text prepared in Word, WordPerfect or AmiPro always go down well. Some bureaux may want you to convert your disks to ASCII format (for the computer literate a simple matter – check your manual). Others can manage it themselves. Copy submitted this way should *not* (on the disk anyway) be submitted in double-spaced format, justified or use a variety of fonts and font sizes. Times New Roman 12-point straightforward is fine. But considerations vary. Check before you begin.

The actual layout of copy is also important. It is best to assume that the bureau will follow the way you've prepared your text more or less slavishly. Get it how you want it from the start and if you think there is any chance of ambiguity write an explanatory note in the margin.

Your first brush with marketing

The link between writing, copy presentation and marketing is more intimate than you might at first think. We will deal with marketing proper in Chapter Fifteen but it is worth considering now a number of seemingly minor points which can eventually affect the sales of your book:

- **Title** So important that in a previous book of mine, *How to Publish Your Poetry*, I devoted a whole section to the subject. Titles chosen by the newcomer to publishing frequently lack impact, are often pretentious and quite regularly act as a real deterrent to sales. As a bookseller, I have come to learn the importance of a good handle – easily pronounceable, easily remembered, direct and specific to the task in hand. A marvellous, self-published cookbook by Bobby Freeman called *First Catch Your Peacock* suffered initially because potential customers did not immediately get the pun and realise it was to do with food. If you are selling a cookbook then you need to say so. Clever titling alone will not do; be succinct. Adolf Hitler's *Mein Kampf* was nearly called *Four-and-a-half Years' Struggle Against Lies, Stupidity and Cowardice*, not the most memorable of lines. Dale Carnegie's amazingly successful *How to Win Friends and Influence People* was almost published as *Friendship and Other Relations with People*, which would have certainly limited its sales. Forty years on, and with few people able to remember the author but all able to recall the title, the book still sells. If you can't be apt, be funny. Hurbert Thurston's *Living Without Eating* and B. J. Ferrell's *Sex After Death* are titles unlikely to be forgotten by customers on their way to the bookshop. The unpronounceable and the rambling will almost certainly fail to come to mind at the cash desk and another sale will be lost.
- **Subtitle** You've kept your title crisp but it doesn't say enough. Fritz Spiegl called his book on newspaperese *Keep Taking the Tabloids!*, which caught the attention, and then appended a subtitle, 'What the Paper's Say and How They Say It', to ensure that the potential buyer knew exactly what he was writing about. Hit with the main title, explain what you are up to underneath.
- **The names on the cover** If there are a group of you working together on the same book try to settle on just one name for the cover. The more authors there are the more chance there is of a buyer getting it wrong and a sale being lost. Keep it simple – elect one of your number as editor. The others can have their moment of glory in full on the title page.
- **The blurb** This brief piece of text resides either on the flaps of the book's dust jacket or, if it is a paperback, on the back cover. Its purpose is to commend the book to potential readers. It is not a place for self-indulgent ego-boosting, irrelevant self-aggrandisement or lies about your achievements. And those full-plate photographs so beloved of first-time poets should be avoided at all costs. A simple, clear, professionally taken black-and-white shot

is best. No trees growing out of your head, no distracting back-grounds and certainly not head and shoulders out of a photo-while-you-wait machine.

Describe your book briefly – its range, its aims, any special features – and don't be afraid to praise your own expertise. As the guide-book author and publisher Hilary Bradt told me, the self-publisher has a huge advantage over the commercial operator here. Self-published books are written and brought out by enthusiasts. They do not sit in the queue in an editor's office. They come out fast and are up-to-date. These are strong selling points. The buyer must be informed – do it on the blurb.

If you are able to get an endorsement of yourself as a writer from someone famous, or perhaps can take a praising comment from a book review of one of your other titles (if you have any), then do so. Be ruthless and unashamed – if nobody has said anything decent about you then say it yourself. Something like 'Acerbic wit and the ability to tell a real story combine in the work of this exciting new fiction writer.' Put the comments between quotation marks but don't attribute them. It is not dishonest. As the writer of those stories you believe it and as their *publisher* you must now learn to say this kind of thing.

The blurb often contains, as a separate paragraph, a few very brief notes about the writer: a list of previous successes in the same field, experience and other achievements. Don't go into too much detail, though: the small things such as your ability to grow roses will not be a selling point on a book about a shipping line. On the other hand, if you've been interviewed by the local radio station make as much as you can of the fact. Being known as a 'broadcaster' lends authority and can lead to sales. Include the year and place of your birth and a bit about where you live now. It is a good idea to be a local writer, so if you have lived somewhere for any length of time – mention it. Become 'local' to as many areas as you can.

The blurb is there to convince the casual browser that the book is worth purchasing. It is an important marketing device. Take time over its composition as more people will read this than will actually read the book. Look at the blurbs of others. Stay up-market – pick Penguin or Picador – as the lower reaches of the mass market tend to be loaded with pulp paperbacks promoted as soap and with a content of similar consistency. On the other hand if this is you then go for it. Art and truth may elude you but you will certainly make cash.

● **House style** In your whole textural presentation you should follow what commercial publishers call a house-style. This means you should adopt a standard for spelling, grammar and layout which should be consistent throughout the work. Which is it: *inquire* or *enquire*? *Catchword* or *catch-word*? *Stop valve* or *stopvalve*? When should you use 'single quotation marks' and when 'double'? Is it *BBC* or *B.B.C.*? When should you abbreviate words? Should foreign phrases like *hors de combat* be set in italics? You should decide and stick to it. I was once criticised for spelling the same word three different ways in a book I self-published twenty years ago. Two versions were legitimate alternatives, the third was the result of bad proof-reading. This error, once it had been publicly spotted, stayed around to haunt me for quite some time. People can be enormously irritated by infelicities of grammar and mis-spellings. Their aggravation, initially over something very small, often ends up obscuring the whole book.

In their time a number of large publishers have brought out handbooks to their own house styles. Not everyone adopts the same standards by any means. Do you correct all Americanisms and appear traditional and stodgy or do you adopt every mid-Atlantic variant that comes your way and turn out text that is just too cool for words? For both clarity and safety I recommend the house style of one of Britain's longest established publishers, the Oxford University Press. Their *Hart's Rules for Compositors and Readers at the University Press Oxford* was originally given away free to enquirers but in response to heavy demand was eventually commercially produced. The latest edition is the thirty-ninth. It covers everything about style you'll want to know and a lot more besides.

Get it checked

Most authors are poor at spelling, punctuation, grammar and self-expression.

Audrey and Philip Ward, *The Small Publisher*

Even those who are grammarians of the old school will still make keying errors and in the blind tiredness that copy preparation induces will invert things, invent things and even leave out whole sections. To cut down on your costs you must ensure that your copy is accurate, error-free, and just as you'd like the book to be. Clear all doubts. Don't ever rely on the bureau or the printer to clarify things for you and certainly do not imagine that the odd slip can easily be corrected later on. It will all cost, in both time and money. Self-publishers are usually of limited means. Read it through, read it through again and then ask a friend or colleague to have a go. Most people will be honoured to be asked. Fresh eyes will find things that you have missed time after time.

Those working on a word processor will inevitably be able to begin their task of checking by using a couple of the program's in-built aids. Most modern word processors have a spell checker which will highlight (and automatically correct) obvious typos as well as querying words with doubtful spellings. Some have grammar checkers which will spot overlong sentences or those which have no main clauses, which start with 'but' or have verbs in the passive voice. These can be of some help, although a check by rule with no consideration of sense often throws up suggestions of doubtful value. Such checking tools are nonetheless good on readability statistics. Mine will tell me my average sentence length (long apparently), the number of syllables I use and if my text is comprehensible to fourth formers. Useful stuff.

How long will my book be?

The number of words you have written is one of your book's vital statistics. Easy to find out if you have a word processor. Amstrad versions require you to spell check the whole text first and then read a word count of work done. PC and Mac versions simply ask you to click the mouse a few times. Computers make it so simple and often overpower us with information. In addition to telling me how many words this book contains my machine also tells me how long I've had the files open on screen, how many pages, characters, lines and paragraphs there are as well as how many times I've made changes.

If you are doing your work on an old typewriter or having someone else key in the text then do not despair. If the work is continuous prose, it is a relatively easy matter to find out how many words it contains. Take a page at random and count the number of words in each of the middle twenty lines. If this happens to contain the end of a paragraph where the line is shorter than the rest then so much the better. Divide your total word count by twenty. This will give you the *average number of words for each line*. Now count the number of typed lines per page over, say, ten pages, all picked at random from the middle of your copy. Divide your total by ten. This will give you the *average number of lines per page*. Multiply the two figures together and you will arrive at the *average number of words per page*. It should be a simple matter now to work out how many you have written in total. Make adjustments for blanks at chapter ends, chapter starts and places where you have decided to include an illustration.

You could, if you wanted to, increase the accuracy of your word count by taking averages from a larger sample, counting twenty pages rather than ten. However, unless the typing is wildly variable the end result won't alter by much. To give you an idea of whether you've worked it out correctly you might like to consider the following:

- A typical paperback novel of 250 pages runs to around 78,000 words.

- A Radio 4 story which, when read out loud, lasts fifteen minutes is about 2,250 words and occupies around seven pages of typed, double-spaced A4 paper.

Finding out how many printed pages your prepared copy will make is nothing like as straightforward. There are a large number of variables in the process of turning a typescript into a book, all of which can affect its length. To get a rough idea refer to your model and work out the average number of printed words per page in that. It will be a simple matter to work out how many pages your copy would occupy if it were printed in a similar way. This assumes that your model is straightforward, contemporary and of a regular size. Many people have come unstuck by basing their calculations on a typeface which is uncommon and on a page size which is uneconomic. When you get around to approaching printers and reprographic bureaux you'll find them quite willing to show you sample pages of different typefaces in various point sizes and will be able to advise you much more accurately on the extent of your proposed book.

If you are concerned only with publishing poetry, then life is a lot simpler. You need only count lines and can ignore word count altogether. If your poems average thirty lines each and a page in your chosen typeface and point size runs to forty then it is an easy matter of printing a poem a page. If you have a number which run a little longer, balance these against your short poems. For example, a fifty-line poem starting on page one will run ten lines into page two. Fill up the remaining space with a twenty-liner or leave it blank if you wish to bulk the book.

The mock-up

The final stage of copy presentation is an actual mock-up of how you imagine your book will be. Commercial publishers concerned with illustrated volumes or books containing a number of charts and tables need to go to some length in their preparation here. Self-publishers with one simple book on their hands do not.

Fold a number of sheets together in approximation of the final page size you require. If this is to be A5 then so much the better. A bundle of plain A4 sheets of copy paper, folded in half, will be quite sufficient. Mark these up to show preliminary matter, title pages and how and where you'd like your text to commence. It is not necessary to represent every page of the text. Unless there are to be illustrations or complex chapter headings, two or three sheets will do. Don't worry about textural accuracy and even if you haven't decided finally on a title it doesn't matter yet – a row of Xs will suffice.

There are two purposes to the mock-up. First it is a practical exercise in layout which will enable you to ensure that, for example, your title page is on a recto and that you've got all the prelims set up in the desired order. Second, and perhaps more important for the amateur, it is an easy way of showing the printer what you intend. Have it between you when you discuss the project. This is the next step: going out to meet the printer. This is where self-publishing becomes real.

8

THE PRINTING PROCESS

It used to be simple but now technology has come along and given us choices.

For the beginner, this is perhaps the most complex stage of the whole business of publishing. There are so many routes from text to book that having to decide which often leads to confusion. There are three distinct processes involved in manufacture:

- *Origination:* the setting of the text in type and the formatting of illustrations.
- *Printing:* the transferring of that type and illustration on to paper.
- *Finishing:* the collecting together of the printed pages to form a book.

Traditionally all three processes are carried out by the same person – the printer. With contemporary practice the industry has become fragmented and it is now quite common and often more economical to employ the resources of a number of different firms. But for the moment let's keep it simple and stick with tradition. Most printers of any size are still capable and usually only too willing to carry out the whole process of book manufacture – origination, printing and then finishing. You deliver your copy, you get back packets of printed books.

Where to start

Let us take a small book of sixty-four pages. It could be fiction, auto-biography, local history or poetry, it doesn't matter. It is small and you are doing it. How many should you produce? A difficult question to answer.

> 'Here's the typescript, let there be a book, two thousand copies should do for the first edition.' The outcome is usually humiliation.
> Roy Lewis and John B. Easson, *Printing and Publishing At Home*

But why? Won't the printer warn you if you are asking for too many? Or give you some idea of what is usual when people do this kind of thing? This, of course, is the problem because, as such, there are no norms in publishing. The chances are that your printer, undoubtedly not without experience in book production, will not be producing titles for individuals every day. How would he know how many copies of your *History of the Bulldog Clip* are likely to sell?

Start by deciding that you are not going to be humiliated by ordering (and paying for) 2,000 copies, selling 200 and having to hide the rest under the bed. Equally you should not be so conservative that your order for 100 (which can make each individual copy very expensive) runs out after a few days and you end up turning potential sales away. Ask yourself some questions. If enough people heard about the book would they buy it? If the answer is yes then start thinking about how you could get them to hear about it. Don't forget that a specialist survey of *Taff Vale Railway Goods Wagons* is unlikely to sell to people other than railway enthusiasts while a *Guide to What to Do on a Wet Sunday Afternoon* has pretty wide potential. Do some market research. Nothing grand. Ask friends and colleagues what they think. Could you sell it to the local school? Ask at the corner shop if they'd stock it. Check the library's opinion. Ask the bookshops.

Deciding quantity is not simple. Certainly it is not worth having anything printed in numbers of much less than 200 and, for the first time round, quantities of more than a few thousand can be a considerable risk. Here are a few typical print runs which may help:

- Pamphlets brought out by a small press   200–300
- Specialist essays in literary criticism   400–800
- Local histories – 'the town in old postcards'   1,000–3,000
- Specialist non-fiction books   1,000–2,000
- New first novels in hardback   800–1,200
- B-format paperback literary fiction   5,000–10,000
- Mass-market paperback thrillers from a new author 25,000
- Booker Prize winners when paperbacked   50,000
- TV promoted cookbooks (Delia Smith,   0.5–1 million
  Madhur Jaffrey)
- Mass-market lead title paperback blockbusters   1 million plus

The print runs of most new books, taken individually, are small. Most writers offset this fact against the knowledge that it is still possible for a complete unknown to come out of the backwoods with a million-seller. What is unlikely is for that book to be done by a self-publisher. Self-publishers almost always get defeated by the difficulties of distribution. Scale is best managed by commercial professionals. The forte of a self-publisher is staking out the market. Their biggest single mistake is to overestimate their potential and make the print run too long. Play safe.

Offset

With the copy to hand and the quantity decided, you are ready to engage a printer. In a sense this is going to be like employing a builder but without the mess. In both cases you will be having somebody make something for you; the art is in explaining exactly how it should be.

Your printer will invariably print by *offset-litho* although there are many other systems available. Some of these, suitable for self-publishers, are described in Chapter Ten. Of particular interest are short-run printing processes based on photocopier technology – notably Rank Xerox's *DocuTech* – but more of this anon. *Offset-litho* is an extremely common and flexible system. It is not a bit like its more traditional predecessor *letterpress* (a form of which Caxton used) where the printing is done by a machine-powered 'rubber-stamp' made of metal. With *letterpress* the text, set backwards, is smeared with ink and pressed on to paper. With *offset* a different principle is used.

A printing plate containing the text is created photographically. The text on this plate is formed from a greasy substance which repels water but attracts ink. The plate is bent around a cylinder and covered, successively, with water and with ink. The text, being greasy, repels the water and picks up the ink. The remainder of the plate, being non-greasy, becomes wet and thereby rejects the ink. Simple. Unlike letterpress, however, the text on the plate is not backwards and needs to be transferred – that is *offset* – on to a second cylinder in order to prevent it being printed in reverse.

Offset machines can be small: there is a version which fits on a desk-top and prints on to pre-cut sheets of A4 paper. They can also be large, rotary web-fed presses printing on to huge rolls of continuous paper, capable of turning out 20,000 copies an hour. There are many other printing processes in use – gravure, screen-printing, thermography and, if you search hard enough letterpress itself for some specialist applications. But ignore them. For book work it will invariably be offset-litho. Ninety per cent of what you find for sale in the shops will have been printed this way.

How to find a printer

Will anyone do? For self-publishers, certainly not. The range runs from back-street, single-operator enterprises to huge factory complexes set on industrial estates. The analogy with the builder will hold – there are those who build walls and fix drainpipes, and others who develop new towns and put up office blocks and opera houses. For a simple book of limited print run you do not need a specialist in four-colour work who prints Sunday supplements; nor on the other hand do you want an individual whose main line is business cards and letterheads. You need a middle-of-the-scale general printer who does a bit of everything – a *jobbing* printer. You can find one by checking local publications in the bookshop and seeing who printed them or by consulting the *Yellow Pages*. Go round and have a look at a few from the outside and if they resemble either a factory or a second-hand shop don't go in. If they seem OK, ask to see samples of the work they do. Check in particular if they do book work and ensure you see an example of something they've done. Ask if they are at all interested in doing work for you.

Your printer will carry out most of the functions of book production – origination, platemaking, collating, binding, printing – on the premises. Some may sub-contract certain tasks to outside specialists but expect them to be able to carry out everything in house if they need to.

Avoid high-street instant print franchises with names like 'Terrifictype' and 'Sprintoprint'. You'll recognise them by their resemblance to building societies – all potted plants and glass. They might be good at invoices and handbills but, despite the smooth manner of their crisply dressed salespeople, they are not the best place for book work. Their pamphlet production, if tolerable, is expensive. Recent estimates that I have obtained were up to twice as much as those I got elsewhere.

Quotations

Quotations are important and it is good practice to obtain a number. It is perfectly proper for you to approach a variety of printers and to discuss the project with each. Ask for a written quotation and if you've specified, say, 300 copies, ask how much extra it would cost to print 400 – in other words the price of a 100 *run-on*. The quotes you receive will vary enormously. Much will depend on how much the printer wants your work. Is there a lot on his order book? Can he make a profit from a number of small jobs, such as yours, or would he be better off with one long run? Has he got some machine capacity spare on a Friday afternoon, enough to run your work? Has he made savings recently on the bulk buying of paper and can he pass that on to you? Are his overheads the same as his competitors? Does he *need* your work? These factors will be reflected in his price. Remember that in the end you will get what you pay for. Do not settle, automatically, for the cheapest. Quality can vary and it is almost impossible to change your mind once the work has begun.

Paper

The paper the book is to be printed on, what the cover is to be made of and how the job is to be bound are very much matters of design, and these are covered more fully in the next chapter. Your printer will be able, however, to offer material from stock. These will inevitably be cheaper than anything he has to buy in specially. They will also be pretty bog standard, making your finished book look pretty much like everything else. Ask for some samples, take them home and consider things. Don't rush to use the first paper that comes to hand.

Placing the order

Be certain your chosen printer understands exactly what you have in mind, and has seen your model, your mock-up and your original copy. Ask him how long it will take and be prepared for his answer to be at variance with the eventual outcome by several weeks. It's a small job; he'll fit it in when he can. If it were a big job the chances are the uncertainty would be worse. Write out your order describing the job required in as much detail as possible. Use all the technical terms you can – filch them from the quotation. Date and price your order, hand over the original, keep a copy for yourself and wait.

Proofs

The first sign you'll receive that the book is under way will be the arrival of the proofs. This used to be a grand two-stage process which enabled authors to check the actual setting (galley proof) and later how the text looked set out as a page (page proof). Advances in technology have altered all that. Today you are more likely to have one bite of the cherry only – the page proof – and that will be that.

In theory, the proofs will have been checked before you see them by the printer looking for his own errors. In practice, to save money, they will often not have been looked at other than, perhaps, by the printer's own spell-checking programs and often not even by those. Expect to find no logic in the mistakes. Sentences will be included twice, and there will be misspellings, transpositions and perhaps, where the setter was distracted by a tea-break or a ringing phone, whole sections completely adrift. Make corrections: they will cost nothing. *Author's corrections*, however, will be charged. These are things which you want changed which are variation from the actual copy. They can stem from becoming victim, through inexperience, of poor layout or deciding to rewrite because suddenly it doesn't sound right. Things can look different once they are set up in type. Don't imagine that you'll be the first person, at proof stage, suddenly to embark on a complete restructure. You will, nonetheless, be charged for the privilege. If you must correct, and it is always better to be right than wrong, then do it now. Corrections once the films or even the plates have been made – if you decide to go to the expense of seeing proofs of these – are difficult to manage and inordinately costly.

Proofs should be corrected using the proof marks set out under British Standard BS 5261. You'll find them listed in the *Writers' & Artists' Yearbook* or you could ask your printer for a set. Traditionally you should correct printer's errors in red and mark up your own in blue. Read through two or three times and, if possible, get a friend to read your original over to you as you follow it on the proof. No matter how meticulous you are, you are bound to let one or two errors get through. Over the years, even the various publishers of the Bible have blundered. In 1631 the King's printers, Barker & Lucas of Blackfriars, managed to get it so wrong that they omitted the word 'not' from the Seventh Commandment. Their 'Thou shalt commit adultery' version of Exodus led to a huge fine and the company's ruin. If you have the time, always read the proofs again.

If the discovered blunders or your own rewritings are extensive and complicated enough it is worth demanding a further set of proofs. Just to check that everything has been carried across. Follow these with care. Quite regularly, new errors creep in and it is not unheard of for the printer to miscorrect or fail altogether to correct errors which you have pointed out. Keep on checking until you feel secure.

Delivery

When the book is ready, expect it to be delivered as a number of brown-paper packets. It is easier if these can be arranged to contain tens or twenties rather than what the printer thinks makes a good bundle which will inevitably be thirty-seven. Ask the printer in advance.

Check for obvious errors. Has the printer followed your instructions and used your choice of paper, cover and binding? Have all the errors you discovered at proof stage been corrected? If all is well, you must settle the bill. Credit is not yours yet; that comes with familiarity and negotiation. For now you must pay on the nail.

9

DESIGN

The designer of printing should be able to visualise the effect of his or her work in finished form before a single type is set.

Herbert Simon, *Introduction to Printing*

Do you want it to look good or to work? It must do both.

Victor Papanek, *Design for the Real World* ·

Small publishers traditionally have *no idea* of book design. Books are books. Design is something you need for a new table lamp or a car. There are blueprints for aeroplanes and ships. There are drawings and plans for houses. But nothing for books. Apart from sorting out the details of how the prelims should run and the illustration for the cover, what else is there to do? It is a difficult concept to grasp.

Design should embrace the entire book; it is the obvious way of controlling the apparent confusion of the process of production. The designer must think of everything, adjusting one aspect against another until the result is all balance and clarity. You will have taken great care over your writing, mixing inspiration with knowledge and polishing the result to perfection; you must take equal care over how the book itself will look.

Don't rush. Details should not be skimped. The first font you come across on the computer is not the best way to do it. Everyday, somewhere, a fresh piece of self-published amateurism reaches the bookshops and makes the situation worse for us all. The spines have no titles; the print is uneven or a cacophony of faces; the lines are cramped so close together that they fall off the page. These books come apart when you pick them up and their pages are so thin you can see your hands underneath. They do their authors no service. They are like soiled clothing; they won't let you in the bar wearing them and at the interview you won't get the job. Your book is an extension of yourself. Make the best of it you can.

Good design is vital. Rather than considering the book as simply a vehicle for what you have to say, try to think of it as an object in its own right. This is what McLuhan insisted on, the medium is the message. Will it feel right when you pick it up? Is the blue cover-board you've chosen appropriate for a book of radical verse? Can you read the title from the other side of the room and is it on the top half of the cover where it won't become obscured in racked displays? Ideal design should attract the eye when the book is among others and should do this without appearing eccentric or odd.

Typefaces

Regarded as almost indistinguishable from each other by the uninitiated, these all have their own distinct personalities. Serif faces, by far the most common in book work, have feet, literally *serifs*, at the base of their descenders. These faces go back to the dawn of type, and are often named after their original designers – Bembo, Garamond, Baskerville, Plantin, Bodoni, Melior and, perhaps the most well-known face of all, Times Roman, named after the newspaper. Those with plain descenders – no feet – are known as grotesque or *sans serif* faces. Franklin Gothic, Helvetica, Futura, Univers and Gill Sans are typical. There is another class of face – display – that is used for headlining, film titling, advertisements and posters. These are generally no use at all for a book's text, although they may look great on a cover. Not all regular faces are readily interchangeable. Some are better for book work than others. Legibility is the aim here. Ask your setter to produce a sample page of your text in a number of different styles to enable you to judge the effect. Generally a sans serif typeface will be less legible than a serif. It is worth spending some time on your final choice. For supreme readability use traditional Times Roman, the perfect solution, but so common you see it everywhere. Better might be Bembo or Palatino although going for some of the more outlandish faces now available – Eurostile Extended or Irish Uncial perhaps – might be taking being different just a bit too far.

A common mistake in amateur book work is to mix wildly different typefaces in an attempt to be stylish. The resultant mess simply jars. The rule is never to mix classes but to contrast only between headline (title) and actual text. Try a serif with a sans serif but limit your choice of faces to two. The aim is ease of reading without tiring the eye. The overall effect across the page should be an even silver-grey.

Not only will your choice of face affect how your book looks; it can also affect significantly how much actual space the text will occupy. Point size, the standard unit of typeface measurement, is unfortunately not an absolute guide to length. Something set in 10-point Roman will occupy a different space from the same thing set in, say, 10-point Futura. Most book work is set in 10-, 11- or 12-point type. And to make things just that little bit more complicated for the uninitiated, type of a particular size is often set into a line space one or two points bigger. 11-point Rockwell set on a 12-point body has more space around it, and therefore is easier on the eye, than the same thing set on an 11-point body. For a clearer explanation of this vast subject check out Charles Foster's excellent *Editing, Design and Book Production Media Handbook* (Journeyman Press) or the classic *Thames and Hudson Manual of Typography* by Ruari McLean.

Typeface choice has come on a thousand-fold with the advent of computer setting. Even the most unillustrious of home word processors usually boasts a dozen or so fonts to select from. But don't be fooled – what you see here will not necessarily be replicated by your printer. Home computers hold only pale imitations of the real thing, often not even bothering to describe them with the same names. Check actual samples before going ahead.

Compare these examples:

This is Bookman Light 10-point, a serif face.

This is Arial 12-point, a sans serif face

This is New Century Schoolbook 11-point, a serif face

This is Dom Casual 18-point, a display face

The first three are thoroughly tried and tested. They are easy to read and do not tire the eye. But they are certainly not the only faces around. Dom Casual is a headline face you could use on a book jacket. It's hand-drawn and modern and you can imagine it being used on price tickets in shops. There are thousands of others like it. As long as your eventual choice for the text is not amazingly eccentric do not worry too much about getting it wrong. 'Nobody ever returns a book to a shop complaining that it is printed in Baskerville 11/12 instead of Bembo 14' as Anthony Blond, in *The Book Book*, quotes Philip Gibbs.

Setting

If it is prose, your text will be set *justified*. This means that the left and right edges will be set parallel to each other, as they are on this page. This is achieved by inserting variable amounts of white space between words, ensuring that each line ends up exactly the same length. It looks tidy and pleasing, and makes the text easier to read. Word processors can effect a form of justification at the click of a mouse, although this will be a far cry from a professionally set text which will have gone through a process of *kerning*, the removal of the rivers of white space a carelessly justified page can be left with.

Unjustified text is where the right-hand edge is left ragged, as in this example. It is the correct way to set poetry and may be used in prose if the space is very narrow (alongside an illustration perhaps) or you are looking for a particular effect. Again word processors get there at a mouse's click – the way it all used to be in the days of the typewriter.

Things to avoid:

● *Widows* – short lines at the end of a paragraph appearing as the first line of the next page. The same sort of effect can occur at a chapter end where one or two lines run on to a fresh page and sit there in splendid and uneconomic isolation.

● *Club lines* – the last line of a page being the first line of a new paragraph.

These problems usually become apparent once the text is set and you see a proof. They can be solved by adjusting the gaps between paragraphs (if you have decided to have any); by altering the *chapter drops* (the distance down the page you should go before commencing text at the start of a chapter); or, if you are doing the setting yourself, by some judicious rewriting. Pad a few sentences out or cut them back.

Page layout

How should it look? Your decision. Remember, though, before starting that no page should be judged on its own merits. At the turn of the century, William Morris's Kelmscott Press drew our attention to the fact that individual pages are not isolated but are invariably part of a double-page spread. They are viewed together and should be designed together. The beginner might imagine that the best place for the typeset, justified block of text is slap in the middle of the page. But placed here, in the geometrical centre, the words will appear to droop. The old masters of book design – Bodoni, Didot, Aldus Manutius – advocated the use of specific proportions. They knew that the margins – the amount of visible white space – were highly significant to the book's ultimate appearance. They should be not equal width but set in the ratio of 2:3:4:5 or 2:3:4:6 for inside, top, outside and bottom respectively. This kind of spacing is, of course, a bit of luxury. Not everyone agrees with it, certainly not the manufacturers of mass-market paperbacks who set their guillotines to fit economic demands, and almost do without margins completely. And there is nothing new in this disagreement either. When Bradford's B. F. Hardwick, 'probably the world's worst binder', was required to produce an octavo ($7^1/2'$ x $5'$) version of Wordsworth's *White Doe of Rylestone*, he simply stuck a quarto ($7^1/2'$ x $10'$) version in the machine and sliced. As a rule I like an outside margin to be big enough to accept my thumb without obscuring the text, although often this is not possible. Try it out on this book. Does it work? Not quite.

In page design measurements judged by the eye are more reliable than those measured with a ruler. Take a typeset block of your text and try moving it around the page a bit to judge the effect. Ideally the length of your line should be two-thirds of the width of the paper, no more (although it seems that in an attempt to cut costs the breaking of this rule is the order of the day). Paragraphs other than the first in any chapter or section should be indented but never by longer than a quarter of the line's overall length. And text, once placed, should register (line-up) well with that on facing pages and be perfectly square with that printed on its reverse. If the text looks dark and closed in maybe some extra space between lines would help. This is known as leading. Try resetting.

Chapter headings are also significant. If these are long and set entirely in upper case (capitals) they may appear quiet and even distinguished but will often be difficult to read because of the uniformity of the letters. What works best is a judicious alternation of large and small letters. Check out a few motorway direction signs. Have you ever seen those set entirely in upper case?

Paper

There are about as many kinds of paper available for printing as there are wines in the world and with a similar range of look and effect. Not all papers are suitable for offset-litho printing and not all for book work. When choosing, seek the advice of your printer.

Paper can be graded according to strength, surface finish, opacity and (importantly) weight. It is measured in grams per square metre: g/m^2 or gsm for short. If the paper weighs too little, print from one side will show through on the other. If it is too heavy, it will not fold satisfactorily to form a page. Papers for book work are usually in the range 85 to 120 gsm and the more they weigh, the more they cost.

Coloured pages are available, often at very little extra cost. Ask for a swatch, a small pad of samples of *readily available, standard* book papers of various types, and in different weights and colours. If economy is vital, find out what the printer has actually got in stock. Any specially ordered paper will cost more. It is worth remembering that if your book is slim, a thick paper will bulk it out. A potential customer will not judge a book's value by its actual extent but more by how thick it appears and how much it weighs. Cash in on this: it is an important consideration. Insert a blank endpaper before the half-title and after the last item of end matter. Use a coloured paper which contrasts with that of the cover itself. At a little extra cost, it will add style and will make you a bigger book.

Binding

The sixty-four-page book is cheapest bound by two machine-inserted wire stitches, that is *stapled*. This is a common and easily accomplished method but it has two disadvantages: staples rust and stapled bindings do not present a squared spine along which the title can be printed. Such books need to be kept face outwards on the shelf in order to remain identifiable. Turn them in and they will vanish. Books that cannot be found do not sell.

These disadvantages can be overcome, but at a price. The wire stitches could be replaced by sewing which, curiously, looks and feels less homemade than machine-inserted staples. A spine can be formed by adopting one of the various systems of *perfect binding* (not a description of how good the method is – a Mr Perfect invented it). These involve trimming away the folded edge of the pages, subjecting the exposed paper to a layer of glue and then drawing on a ready folded cover. There is a limit to the thinness of books which can be successfully bound this way. If in doubt include a few blanks or use heavier paper; your printer will advise.

Covers

The choice is wide. Books have been covered in everything from ceramic tiles to human skin, although card is more usual. For an inexpensive sixty-four pages, it will be best to use standard art-board, available in a range of colours and finishes. Again ask for samples and details of costs. What you print on this cover is very important, as half the book purchases in the UK are made on impulse. The factors which clinch the final sale are various but in order that they may be allowed to come into play *the customer must first be encouraged to pick up the book*. How? A good title, an interesting subject, a known author, and of overriding importance, *an arresting cover*. Design and presentation must demand that the book be investigated. How you do this on a tight budget is difficult but not impossible. The problems of printing illustrated work and using display type are dealt with in Chapter Eleven. For now suffice it to say that a picture is generally better than mere typography and a dash of colour can make all the difference. Avoid red, which can get bleached out quite dramatically by sunlight.

Opinions differ widely as to what makes for a good front jacket. Artists like art, booksellers like commercial design. What is often overlooked is that covers should serve two purposes: they should both reflect the content and sell the book. Illustration should on no account obscure the title: cover art should not be an end in itself. It is no good having a book about sailing the Norfolk Broads illustrated by a Dali-like piece of surrealism which relegates the author's name and title to a line across the bottom set in 12-point type. Be bold but appropriate. Be legible. Keep it looking like a book.

The best examples of contemporary cover artwork, probably in the world, may be found on a selection of recent British paperbacks. Study these to see how it can be done. On a restricted budget, however, the effects you can aim for will of necessity be much less sophisticated.

Illustrations can be obtained from a number of sources. You can use photographs so long as these are from good, high-contrast originals. Do not try to copy something cut from a newspaper as reproduction is always poor. Do not use a portrait of yourself either. Unless you are a media personality, such affectation is best left to the stars.

If you are to use original artwork, you will either need to create it yourself or commission an artist. These are best found socially although working with friends can prove embarrassing if you don't like what they turn out. Do not assume that anyone with a flair for drawing will be able to help. Book covers are not simply illustrations with titles incorporated. They are advertisements for the book.

Since it can be argued that the cover is at least as important as the content, this might be the one occasion on which the shoestring publisher should employ a professional designer. You can find one through *Yellow Pages* or ask your printer. He may have a designer on his staff or regularly use a local freelance. Most of the designers I know will offer you a first consultation free of charge in order to give you some idea of the possibilities and the costs.

There remains the problem of colour. To stand out a cover must have some, even just a dash, but providing it can prove disproportionately expensive. There are a few short cuts you might consider, all of which have been successfully tried out by small and self-publishers. Which you use will depend on how big your edition is to be and how dextrous and artistic you are.

● Bill Griffiths, a tireless innovator running his own Amra Editions, published his collected poems a few years back. Colour was added to the pre-printed titling by impressing the cover with a poster-paint-loaded cellular sponge. The result was an eye-catching rainbow swirl, different for each book.

- Poet Chris Ozzard and local historian Roger Lee Brown have both explored the buying in of pre-printed illustration. They have produced books with postcards depicting local scenes or gallery art stuck to the covers. The effect is reassuringly professional. Permission to use a card in this fashion is obtained from its publisher and acknowledgement made on the verso of the title page. Most postcard publishers regard the practice as good advertising and are only too glad to sell their cards in bulk. Some even offer a discount.

- The hand-colouring tradition of William Blake is worth considering, although it can be hugely time consuming. The Red Sharks Press edition of *A Child's Guide to Ian MacMillan* has a black-and-white cartoon on the cover which press operator Chris Mills finishes in felt pen. On each copy, Ian MacMillan's shirt is different – avoids monotony, says Mills.

- Some publishers have explored the colour photocopier as a device for cover production. If your edition is small enough colour repro this way can be just about economic. Copiers are able to output on thin card. Another possibility is to copy a number of times on to the same sheet and then cut and paste.

- Other methods are to spray-paint spot-colour via a stencil. Use car paint if you like, which dries quickly but can make you high if you use a lot of it in a confined space. Colour can be potato-blocked, splashed on, brushed on, or shapes can even be cut from pre-coloured sheets and stuck into place. Such techniques inevitably require the edition to be very small and for there to be space available in which to lay out all the covers to dry. Be careful where you put them. Rigby Graham and associates at the Pandora Press used the attic of the old rectory at Aylestone to dry work for their edition of *Fingal's Cave*. In an unexpected spell of spring sunlight the floor's woodworm hatched and flew off: over 100 sheets of carefully printed paper were irrevocably peppered with holes.

Whichever way it is approached – from do-it-yourself silk-screen if you have the technique, to paying the printer to at the very least contrast title and illustration – colour is important. Afford it if you possibly can.

Clear, annotated book design is a way of avoiding the yawning chasm between your idea of what the end product will look like and what the printer will actually produce. Plan ahead. Write your specification down.

10

HOW TO MAKE IT CHEAPER

It is too expensive. Possibly the greatest deterrent to becoming a self-publisher is the size of the print bills you have to face – it comes as a revelation that the actual cost of having things printed is so high. Suddenly, the price of a new hardback stops sounding exorbitant and the £6.99 on the back of the latest Penguin seems unassailably cheap. But before you give up the idea, there are a number of points worth thinking about:

1   Are you sure you are requesting standard page sizes: pocket paper-back (A format); crown octavo or large crown octavo (paperback B format); A5 or demy octavo? Is the setting regular? Are you certain you are not demanding something out of the ordinary for the cover?

2   Could you use cheaper paper? There is always something to be had which costs a bit less, coming right down the scale to newsprint. Have a look at some samples, preferably with print on them. Examine these carefully to see how much of the text shows through from one side to the other. Could you put up with what you find?

3   Could you make the book shorter? If it is poetry or short fiction this is a simple matter of dropping an item. If, on the other hand, the book is continuous narrative could you edit it down? For it to make any real difference to your costing, text would have to be dropped in units of at least four pages. You could make up for the apparent scarcity of content by using a heavier weight of paper.

4   Could you lower the book's unit cost? This is easy: you print more. Unit costs for printing-machine time, paper and finishing operations are relatively fixed (although see Chapter Twelve on short-run specialists). Origination costs are a one-off, no matter how many copies you produce; they are the same for ten copies as they are for ten thousand. The greater the number of copies you can spread them over, the less *per unit* they will become. Beware, though, of the rising *total* print bill. These are the economics of selling to a mass market. If you can sell enough copies then the retail price will fall. If you begin with a cheap enough price then there is every pos-sibility that you will sell enough. Despite this simple equation, books will always turn out to be harder to shift than the relatively inexperienced person realises. If your unit costings seem intractable

67

do not simply increase your print run in order to bring them under control. Don't count on your title taking off. *Never* order more copies than you reasonably think you can sell.

5   If the total print bill is beyond your reach don't be badgered into reducing it by ordering *fewer* books. The principles of reducing cost outlined above will work in reverse. The £15 pamphlet will have few buyers.

Doing some of it yourself

You'll have realised now, if you didn't before, the truth of the old adage that time equals money. The way to make big savings in book production is to do parts of the work yourself.

> The art is to do what you are good at and enjoy, then delegate the rest.
>
> Audrey and Philip Ward, *The Small Publisher*

Reapproach your printer and ask for the quotation to be broken down into detailed stages. From this it will be possible to work out the price of each process and the amount you can expect to save if you manage to carry out some of it yourself. Not all printers will be willing to accommodate you; their original quotes may be based on doing the complete job or they may be secretive as to the actual cost of specific stages. Ask anyway. See what room there might be for manoeuvre. Printers are quite used to customers getting involved.

You may decide to buy and supply your own paper. This is a long shot really – approaching a mill directly usually ends up with the self-publisher paying *more* not less. If you did manage it your printer may decide to recoup part of his loss of mark-up on paper supply elsewhere in the costs for your job. You will have to balance the overall saving, which would now be quite small, against the extra effort involved in having to deal with the mill.

What other parts of the process are worth attempting? Amateurs have been known by dint of effort to do the lot. Nothing is impossible, nothing arcane. The British Printing Society reports one member producing splendid work on a hand-built wooden press, set up in a bedroom. Anthony Hopkinson makes his own paper out of newsprint and starch pulped in a kitchen liquidiser, while a large number of self-publishers do their own finishing. Can you put up a bookshelf? If you can you should be able to make the book to go on it. Much depends on skill or, more specifically, the time you have available to acquire it.

Origination

This is where the really big savings can be made. As we have already seen, a considerable proportion of the costs of any book is incurred before a single plate has had ink put on to it. If you have skills in this area or own equipment and can ignore the cost of your own time then your books will work out costing you considerably less.

Typesetting, once invariably carried out in-house at the printer, can now be readily done outside. Or you can do it yourself. If you can minimise the number of *key strokes* others need to do on your behalf the savings can be significant. There are a number of possible options:

● In the simplest instance text set on a word processor can be cut and stuck into place on sheets marked up to represent the page layout of the book. This process – known as *paste-up* – produces camera-ready copy (CRC) from which the printer will make the plates. Use Spray Mount as your adhesive (although Pritt Stick will do) and remove any blemishes with a correcting fluid such as Tipp-Ex. If you need to bring anything specific to the plate-maker's attention this can done with a blue chinagraph pencil. Blue markings are invisible to the camera. But take care. It is quite easy to misalign things. The eye becomes unreliable. Check with ruler and set-square; a small drawing board would help. Lines which deviate from true by more than half a millimetre are noticeable. Two or three millimetres out and you'll look like a sinking ship.

    The other big difficulty is getting pages in the wrong order. Discuss the plan with the printers and if they're willing to work with you this way. Most will be. They'll advise on *imposition* – which pages go where, how they should be numbered and which way up they should be.

    Imposition is an important part of paste-up, the exact details of which will depend on the size and format of the printer's machine. Small, desk-top lithos will print on ready-cut-to-size A4 sheets. Imposition for these is straightforward. It may be that your printers will use a larger machine capable of running off the equivalent of two, four or eight A4 sheets simultaneously. The standard unit in book production is a *signature* of thirty-two pages. These can often be printed on a single large sheet which is then folded, cut and trimmed. So long as the imposition was carried out correctly in the first place, the pages will run neatly in order. Discover which system your printer uses and follow the plan you'll be given. To find out more read mathematician Harry Mulholland's logical explanation in his self-published *Guide to Self-Publishing* (Mulholland Wirral).

The photographic plate made from your CRC will show up every blemish, smudge and fingerprint you've left on it. Go over the copy in a strong light and with correcting fluid paint out every suspicion of a mark.

If you have no word processor you can still manage things on a decent typewriter. Clean the daisy-wheel first, make sure you use a brand new ribbon (preferably carbon film) and, to avoid smudging, remove the finished sheets from the roller with the greatest of care. Justification, of sorts, can be achieved by typing the text twice. On the second time round, if needed, you insert appropriate amounts of extra space into your lines. The best place is after stops or colons.

● Another more expensive possibility is for you to set your text using a word processor and then have a reprographic bureau convert it into pages. Bureaux are regular intermediaries between client (you) and printer. They present a number of opportunities:

a) Your word-processed text can be sent to them on disk where it will be reset as pages. This will be done without the need for expensive rekeying. The set pages, once proofed by you, will be output via laser printer on to ordinary paper from which you can prepare your CRC. If you do this it might be worth asking for output on a smooth finished paper which will make for a finer image. Output can also be made in the form of a *bromide* – a high-quality print which will give even better reproduction. Bromides need to be prepared photographically (rather than laser printed) and therefore are more expensive. Bureaux can also accept text in hard-copy form. This they can rekey for you (expensive) or if it is sufficiently clean, i.e. clear and without handwritten correction, scan the text directly into their computers. Again there is a cost involved but nothing like as much as for a total retype.

b) A second option is for the bureau to output your work not on a regular laser printer with its variously ragged typeface reproduction but via what is known as an imagesetter. Laser printers make up each letter from a matrix of tiny dots. Current standard is around 600 dots per inch (dpi) and regarded by many as quite sufficient for book work. At least one professional publisher of my acquaintance uses nothing else. But for high-quality work, especially for anything to be run alongside illustrations or on art paper, text set at between 1,200 and 2,540 dpi is the only option. The machine used here will be an imagesetter. Output, which is expensive, will be on the same kind of photographic material used for a bromide. Imagesetters work at the top end of the market and are by no means standard equipment everywhere. If you intend using this kind of output check with bureau (and printer) first.

c) A third possibility is for output to avoid paper completely and go straight to film. We are in the future here – the way all reproduction is going. The printer avoids a further stage in the plate-making process by not having to use a camera. Your text – page set by the bureau and proofed before output – is run directly as positive film which is then manually imposed by the printer before creating the plate.

d) To get even nearer an instant book the bureau could set your text and then format it into pages using an imposition program. This would avoid the printer having to get his hands dirty at all. No manual imposition, just a piece of film from which to make a plate. And why not go further? Why have film – why not go directly from computer screen to plate? Such systems exist. But for first-time self-publishers perhaps a little sophisticated.

e) There are a variety of other ways in which using a bureau may offer you savings (or present you with a more flexible method of production). If your home computer has a modem, suitably encapsulated text can be sent directly to the bureau down the line. No disks. Proofs for correction can be returned to you the same way. Bureaux can be invaluable for scanning in and placing illustrations (more of this later). They also have good connections with the printing trade and, if you need them to, will be well placed to advise on competent and appropriate choices for the carrying out of your work.

● The radical alternative to all this is to go back to the days of the scriveners and copy the text by hand. This can look extremely twee unless done well and I personally cannot be bothered to force myself through page after page of calligraphed autobiography or recipes written in copperplate. Famous poets are quite fond of having the occasional poem produced in facsimile of their handwriting. These are done in limited editions and usually sell well to collectors. I can't imagine many wanting to *read* their poetry this way.

Covers

At its simplest, a cover is a design which incorporates the title and author's name in a form strong enough to demand that the reader pick the book up. At the economic end of the presentation spectrum this will be one-colour ink on plain art board (see Chapter Nine for ways of cheaply introducing spot colour). Avoid white: everyone who hasn't thought about it leaves their cover white and unless they have been laminated these get grubby very quickly. Try for orange, green or bright yellow.

Your illustration will be appropriate and eye-catching with lots of crisp contrast. To reproduce clearly the original *must* be in black-and-white. Avoid pencil drawings, shades, washes, tones and shadows – these cost extra to produce. Skip photographs altogether. Make it simple and punchy. A visual set within a square border, placed upper centre and surmounted by title text in a large point size can be very effective.

Set your name and your title in a clear, non-fussy display face. Whatever you do avoid 'olde English' black lettering which most people admire but almost certainly find difficult to read. You can provide your own *headlining*, as titling is called, by either using dry-transfer lettering or text from your word processor. Computer-produced text is much simpler to set and to manipulate. Move headline and illustration around until they look right and then stick them down.

This aspect of publishing has always caused me problems. I'm prone to changing my mind so often that after a few hours of paper shuffling I have less idea of what works than when I started. The solution I've contrived is to leave what seems a reasonable version, set up but unglued, on the floor and spring in on it an hour or so later to see how it looks. If it has enough impact in that first glance, then we are on. This is how bookbuyers see things – all over in a matter of seconds.

The back cover will need preparation at the same time as the front and should incorporate the blurb (see Chapter Seven). Good effect can be gained by repeating the display setting of your title and name in a smaller point size and by using a continuation of the main illustration.

Do the cover well. Spend time over it. Make sure the typography is squarely aligned. This is what the customer sees first.

Finishing

Labour-intensive tasks such as pulling each of the eight sheets plus a cover of a sixty-four-page book together are readily taken over by the amateur. Done by hand, the material will lack the marks of the mechanical collator but this matters little – the folds will be human, the sheets will be single and the stapling will be reasonable if not absolutely precise.

Set the piles of paper at the edges of a table and start walking round and round it. With a rubber fingerstall on your thumb, pull a sheet off each stack. It can take a whole evening and make you dizzy. Treat it like harvest time. Get friends and neighbours to help, down some cider and sing a few songs as you circle. You might as well enjoy saving cash.

Stapling follows tapping the pages and cover of each book square. Professionals use a mechanical *jogger* for this. You'll need a long-arm stapler with enough reach to cross an A5 sheet. Standard office models will not do it. You can rent machines (including power models) at some hire shops or try borrowing one from your printer. As a last resort you can buy one but typically for such equipment they cost incredibly more than you'd expect.

Folding is just sore thumbs. There are no short cuts and you have to press hard.

The final finish involves trimming the fore-edge square in a guillotine. This is not essential but if you can do it, a crispness will be imparted to your production that it would otherwise lack. Guillotines of sufficient size to be of any use are amazingly expensive. Again it is a case of tapping the printer or back to the hire shop. If you are going to bother you might as well get it right.

An alternative to stapling is sewing which, if done neatly, looks classier and does not rust. You'll need a heavy-gauge needle and a lot of time. Guillotining can be replaced with a Stanley knife, a steel rule and some arm-work. Trimming with scissors will not do the job at all.

Other ways of saving cash

Duplicate

Go back in time and use a duplicator. The once ubiquitous office Gestetners and Roneos (or their predecessors, the heady-smelling Bandas) can still be found if you look hard enough. The duplicator was known as the mimeograph in America and was the first device that the non-specialist could use without too much instruction and at a relatively low cost. Its appearance sparked the mimeo revolution, throwing up a host of small literary presses and a bewildering variety of specialist little magazines. Duplicators worked by cutting letters into a wax stencil using a typewriter with the ribbon removed. The cut stencil was wrapped around a drum and ink squeezed through on to paper beyond. This paper could not be smooth finished but had to be thick and textured in order to absorb the ink. Duplicated booklets often had the feel of beer mats as a result. If you have access to such a machine and, in particular, the supplies of specialist stencil, ink and paper required then you could still give it a go. Ian Templeton's book, *Publish it Yourself and Make it Pay* (Pikers Pad) describes the process in detail.

Photocopy

The duplicator vanished when the cheap, efficient office photocopier arrived. The plain paper copier completely changed our approaches to print. No mess, no wet ink, no plates or stencils to prepare. Put in an original, press the button and out comes a copy, clear, non-smudgeable and dry. Hard to tell, at a glance, from the same page reproduced by offset-litho. Copiers enlarge and reduce, and those with fitted hoppers and sheet feeders can copy a whole sheaf of papers, front and back, in order. Sounds like a self-publisher's dream but the economics of using it on any scale remain a problem. The hundredth copy you produce costs the same as the first. Fine for short runs but for anything above 150 copies formal offset-litho is the obvious alternative.

What are the options for buying or renting a machine yourself? Bob Cobbing, who owns a photocopier, reckons that his costings prove the system worth investigating. A copier will cost at least £1,000 to buy, plus £300 or so annual service charge – the machines break down a lot. It is possible to lease for less or to buy second-hand. The huge advantage of owning a machine is that the cost per copy, depending on overall use, is usually under 1p. Compare that with the charges of between 5p and 10p made by high-street print shops.

To enjoy fully the photocopier's advantages, the self-publisher needs to approach the system via the back door, either through a contact who has access to a machine or via other means. I have heard a tale (which I by no means recommend emulating) of a West Wales publisher who, armed with his own paper to confound possible charges of stealing, walked into the town hall and, being indistinguishable from any other local government officer, was allowed use of the Xerox unmolested. He said the trick was to go in wearing shirtsleeves; that way they think you belong. Do not, unless you are interested only in producing copies in single figures, pay commercial copy-shop or library slot-machine rates. Such charges are designed to attract the document copier rather than the small publisher of books.

Home letterpress

Once the only way of producing fine-looking amateur editions. Horace Walpole at Strawberry Hill did this, although he employed workers to run the machines for him. Virginia and Leonard Woolf ran their small machine on a table top. This was the start of the Hogarth Press, possibly the most significant act of self-publishing this century. Parlour printing is still possible although, unless you are a real enthusiast, it can be a vastly demanding and messy process. Letterpress, which involves setting each individual letter by hand and then carefully inking up the resultant page before pressing it on to paper is also very slow. But if you are interested try and hunt down a second-hand Adana machine, one of the few pieces of letterpress equipment designed for use by amateurs. Letterpress these days is the province of the expensively produced private press where paper, binding and setting combine to give us some of the finest examples of the book available. Check some of the editions still being produced at Gregynog Press (Newtown, Powys). For more information on the subject check Roy Lewis and John B. Easson's *Publishing and Printing at Home* (David & Charles) or *Herbert Simon's Introduction to Printing – the Craft of Letterpress* (Faber & Faber). Both out of print now but they should be available through your library.

Home litho

Offset equipment comes in a variety of sizes including small 'desktop' models, originally designed for the office market. Essentially these are no different from their bigger relatives other than in the size of the paper they can print. Offset machines are complex: vastly more so than an Adana. If a letterpress is a pushbike then a small offset is a 1,000 cc motorbike. This analogy holds true with both speed of printing and cost of purchase. Offset machines cost thousands and home printers may find themselves buying a small commercial print shop rather than equipment for a hobby.

A small offset is of little use on its own – it requires plates with which to print. It is possible to pay for these to be produced for you or you could buy your own plate-maker. Set aside several hundred pounds. More effort is needed to maintain offset equipment, although decent results are on the whole easier to obtain. Buying second-hand should be undertaken with care. An old letterpress, unused for decades, can be revitalised; an offset machine left to rust in a garage is probably beyond repair. More information can be had by reading *The Blueprint Handbook of Print and Production* by Michael Barnard, John Peacock and Charlotte Berrill (Blueprint).

Bind at home

If the book is sixty-four pages or less, centre or side stapling will usually be sufficient. Home printers, concerned with the craft of the book, often hand-sew. With more substantial works, perfect binding can be achieved given access to a hand press or at worse a pair of flat wooden boards and something to weigh them down. Additional requisites are PVA glue and an electric fire to speed the drying process.

Some home printers develop a parallel interest in hardback bookbinding – a craft equal in complexity to their printing. The technique is best described in *The Thames and Hudson Manual of Bookbinding* by Arthur W. Johnson and *The Craft of Bookbinding – a Practical Handbook* by Eric Burdelt (David & Charles).

Get together

I've already touched on the idea of carrying out some of the printer's sub-contracting yourself and explained the possible problems you could encounter if you try to buy your paper independently. However collectives can often succeed in this field. A joint approach from three or four self-publishers may amount to an order large enough to qualify for a saving. Societies such as the Association of Little Presses and the British Printing Society (see Appendix One) already bulk buy on behalf of their members. If you are unable to get in touch with other local self-publishers, such organisations may be worth joining for this purpose alone.

A further advantage of society membership, particularly of the ALP, is the possibility of communal access to equipment. Small publishers often own guillotines, electric staplers and photocopiers. It may also be possible by enrolling in an evening or extra-mural class to gain access to school or college equipment. George Bradt, an innovative self-publisher of works on backpacking, solved the twin problems of lack of cash and lack of skill by going to work for a printer. He worked, unpaid, learned the craft and while he was there published *Backpacker's Africa* and *Backpacking in Peru and Bolivia* for the cost of the materials alone.

Self-publishers often need to adopt the less obvious approach. For many this is the only way.

11

PROCEEDING UPWARDS: HOW TO IMPROVE ON THE BASICS

... no distress in elegance

Gertrude Stein

For some writers, the sixty-four-page pamphlet, produced as cheaply as possible, is no worthwhile target. Why buy a Lada when you can have a Mercedes or a Porsche? To the eyes of many, the content of a book can only be as good as the form in which it is presented. Tradition demands fine bindings and quality papers – life is not all bargain basement. There are better ways of doing things than wire-stapling your autobiography between flimsy boards.

It should be a matter of economics. Can you afford a better production? Will the book still sell to its targeted audience at a higher price? Does this matter? Will you subsidise it for the pleasure of seeing it looking right? It is an easy matter to ask the printer to improve the quality but before giving *carte blanche* consider where improvements can most readily be effected.

Paper

A huge difference can be made to the look, feel, style and even smell of a book when the paper is improved. A concomitant of quality paper is the way it lies when the book opens and the way it moves when you turn the page. Ask to see samples of blade-coated cartridge papers. Check off-whites. Have a look at something a little heavier than the standard 80 gsm.

Print

Ignore litho which, beyond a certain point, makes one book of high-quality sixty-four pages indistinguishable from the next. Hunt hard among the specialist printers and go back to letterpress. The settings are different, the papers are different, the *look of the print on the page*, pushed there not rolled on, adds quality and style. The essence of printing for the private presses of Britain and Ireland is letterpress. For these bastions of quality, offset-litho cannot be considered a possibility at all. But expect to pay, and expect to pay a lot.

Cover board

The most dramatic, immediate improvements to any publication can be achieved by upgrading their covers. It is an obvious expediency to drop the regular art board and go for something better. There are any amount of possibilities so ask to see the range available. Bear in mind that an expensive white cover will become shop soiled just as quickly as a cheap one and that card will not happily hand-fold around more than sixty-four pages.

Gloss finish

The way to pick up the display lights and to shrug off fingerprints. Gloss can be added as a clear varnish by the printers, running it on like ink, or the board can be glossy to begin with. The best effect is achieved by having the books *laminated* after printing. This is a distinct process, usually subcontracted, and can be extremely effective. Books are machine-covered with a thin material not dissimilar to cling film. For a comparatively small extra charge you get a high gloss cover of professional appearance which will add both style and class to your book.

Colour

As I've said before, the single most effective addition to a cover, and one which should be invested in if at all possible, is colour. Full-colour covers can be produced by most (but not all) printers. The method in common use is known as the *four-colour process* where all colours present in the original are mixed from different combinations of yellow, magenta, cyan (blue) and black. The four printing plates necessary are made from the original illustration by exposing it to the camera through different colour filters.

Colour work is expensive because it requires more machine time, but it is worth buying. Less expensive effects can be obtained by printing in other than black on a coloured board or by printing solid colour on a white board and having the title *reversed out* (that is printing colour on the cover, leaving the title white).

Illustrations

The highly illustrated book is the mark of advanced printing technology. It is inappropriate for some works but an enhancement to others. Poetry can work well with the occasional line drawing; fiction too. Local history and guidebooks are virtually impossible without photographs, maps and sketches.

For the purposes of print, illustrated matter can be divided into two types – line and tone.

- Line is anything that can be reproduced in straight black-and-white with no gradations. It includes pencil-and-ink drawings in outline, solid colour, shading representd by dots or cross-hatching and any illustrated matter *which has been previously been printed*.

- Tone is anything that involves shading, shadow and graduating colour. This usually means photographs (black-and-white as well as colour) but can include charcoal drawings, and illustrations made by collage or with paint, crayon and felt pen.

Line illustrations present no problems for reproduction and are pasted-up into the camera-ready copy along with the text. Tone illustrations have to be processed first. The system is based on an optical illusion. Gradations of shade are converted to dots by photographing the original through a mesh-like screen. The resulting *halftone*, as the prepared illustration is called, conveys the impression of shadow and shade by a varying of the density and size of the dots. At its crudest, this can readily be seen in newspaper photographs. Light areas have few dots; dark areas have many more, densely packed. The eye doesn't register the dots unless it looks for them – it sees a photograph. In much the same way, when watching television, the eye ignores the 625 lines which make up the screen.

Illustrated material for reproduction is generally prepared separately from text and is incorporated into the page at film stage rather than pasted into the artwork. A process known as PhotoMechanical Transfer (PMT) enables screened prints of your illustrations, made to the required size, to be prepared in advance. These are then stuck directly into the artwork which gives you the advantage of seeing how things will turn out. PMT is also useful if your original is regarded as too valuable to send to the printer. A rough idea of how things will look can also be had by using a zoom photocopier to produce rough examples of illustrated material at the size you need. These can be loosely affixed to the artwork to show the printer where the original is to go.

If you are lucky enough to work with a computer running appropriate software and have access to a sophisticated enough scanner most of the above processes can be forgotten. You can scan your illustrations direct to your screen, manipulate them as required and then drop them directly into the correct place in your text. If you are using a bureau then this route is one you may care to explore.

The following are some points to notice:

- Artwork for reproduction which is not incorporated directly into the paste-up should be marked on its reverse with caption and intended position. Call each piece *pic* and indicate both page number and name of publications. 'Pic A, page 35, *My Part in Thatcher's Downfall* by D. Coombs.' Avoid writing this directly on to the pic's reverse in ball point as the impression may show through. Use a sticky label.
- Captions need to be typeset and should be clearly indicated either on your copy or assembled on to a single sheet, set, and then pasted into your artwork as appropriate. Captions can be printed beneath or to the side or actually across the illustration to which they refer. If this is dark, as is likely, text will need to be reversed out. Indicate this on the copy.
- If only part of an illustration is required for reproduction, refrain from actually cutting up the original. Write directions on the reverse or preferably attach a sheet of tracing paper as an overlay, ruled up to indicate the area for reproduction. These rules are *crop marks*.
- Reduction or enlargement of any illustration always occurs in proportion. To see what this will be draw a box to represent the exact outside dimensions of the original. Connect the bottom-left and top-right corners with a diagonal line and extend this upwards, beyond the box. Any changes in dimension will always occur along this line.

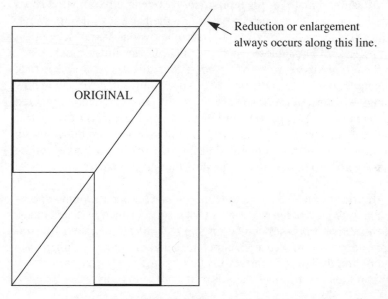

Reduction or enlargement always occurs along this line.

ORIGINAL

- Reduction will sharpen detail; enlargement may blur it.
- A glossy photograph with clear black and whites reproduces best. Black-and-white reproduction from a colour original is possible but less successful.
- Previously screened illustrations, i.e. those which have been printed somewhere already, will require no further processing but inevitably, as reproductions will involve copying of an original, there will be some loss of quality.
- Illustrations may be reproduced as they are, enclosed in a box or a border or run right across the margins and off the page, which is known as *bleeding*. Indicate which style is required. Bleeding can add to the costs.
- Almost the first thing to remember with black-and-white litho work: the colour blue does not reproduce at all.

How to publish a bigger book

Successions of words are so agreeable.

Gertrude Stein

Sixty-four pages is limiting. Your novel may be 100,000 words, your guide to easy parachuting may be 200 pages long. Such ventures require a much larger initial investment and a great deal more co-operation between publisher and printer. The more money and time you risk, the much larger your knowledge should be of the business in which you are dealing. The more there is to do the more there is to go wrong. Study the subject. When you have finished this book, read some of the others mentioned in Appendix Two. Of particular importance are Audrey and Philip Ward's *The Small Publisher* (Oleander), Hugh Williamson's *Methods of Book Design* (Yale), *Copy-Editing: the Cambridge Handbook* by Judith Butcher (Cambridge University Press) and the indispensable *Editing, Design and Book Production* by Charles Foster (Journeyman Press).

Not all printers will be suitably equipped to handle production of a bigger book – ask. Make certain you see samples of previous work done. If in doubt write to the British Printing Industries Federation, 11 Bedford Row, London WC1R 4DX (0171 242 6904) which produces a catalogue of book and learned journal printers. 'All are experts in their field, and are happy to answer your questions on book production even though you may not have immediate need of their services.'

Larger books need different bindings: sixty-four pages is near the limit for successful wire-stitching or staples. The trade standard is the square-spined paperback produced either by perfect binding (see Chapter Nine) or by sewing individual thirty-two-page *sections* of the book together and pulling a glued pre-folded cover onto the resultant volume. Naturally the sewn and glued paperback is the stronger and is more expensive to produce.

Alternatives include wire or plastic spiral bindings which look untidy and do not stack well. Such books open perfectly flatly but this advantage (apart from in the case of road atlases) is outweighed by the difficulty in printing anything on the spine. Spine titling is absolutely vital to prevent the work vanishing when shelved.

Traditional hardback bindings, once done in leather, are now board or board-backed cloth. For some writers this is the only mark of publication there is – paperbacking is considered to be an apprenticeship. However, such productions can boost costs considerably. Not only has the case to be formed and the title stamped on to it, but a dust-jacket has to be designed, printed and paid for. These charges must be passed on and can result in the retail price more than doubling. If you decide to take this kind of financial risk, it really is a matter of knowing just who your intended audience is. A compromise is to consider producing a paperback trade edition and to satisfy vanity and the libraries with a limited run of perhaps 100 hardbacks.

It is still possible to carry out parts of the production process yourself, as outlined before. But as the venture is bigger, and we hope better, it is important to take extra care. If you have never pasted-up copy before then begin on a pamphlet. A 200-page guide to walking the Ridgeway is an expensive book on which to learn by your mistakes.

When ordering print, check the estimate to ensure that it specifies exactly what you want. Check the fine print to find out under what circumstances surcharges and extras are payable and do your best to avoid them. Place your order in writing. Try to establish a good relationship with the printer. Ensure you both understand what is expected – this is the best insurance against things going wrong.

12

CAN'T COPE?

This all seems too much. Self-publishing is such a complex and variable a process that the book you want seems to be forever beyond your grasp. But fear not: you do not *need* to do everything yourself. Assistance can be bought. Professional, marketable publication can be achieved with tears and without exploitation. But there is a cost.

Designers

The first fall-back will be to talk to a professional designer, who understands the relationship of text to page, who knows about typography and who understands papers, their quality and the effect they can have on finished product. Designers have long, hands-on experience with setting systems, cover layouts and finishing processes. They know (or should do) just what deep-green ink will look like on an off-white 100 gsm cartridge. They are familiar with how photographs will appear, enlarged, cropped or run as a duotone on the cover. They know how chapters should start and understand indenting, margins, widows, orphans and kerning. In short, they know how books work and can help you put yours together. Designers deal with the visual. Don't expect help from them on the written text, or on how you've set this together. You still need to prepare a dummy. But once a designer is employed the headaches, if you are getting them, can be made to lift.

The bread-and-butter work of many designers is the corporate brochure, the promotional campaign run by the local manufacturer, the display adverts placed everywhere by the chainstore, or the glossy pamphlet you find shoved through your door telling you what's on at the leisure centre during the holidays. Not all designers handle book work as a matter of course, but they all know print. Designers can act as fine intermediaries between you, the reprographic bureau and the printer. They know prices and can advise on the most economic contacts to follow. A good designer will get you a professional-looking book, capable of standing alongside anything on the shelves at Waterstone's. The content and how it sells will, naturally, still be up to you. But as an insurance that the job will work, designers can be invaluable. Expect to pay for their services. Books produced this way always work out more costly than those you do completely yourself.

Where do you find one? The Graphic Designers section of your local *Yellow Pages*, stuck in there neatly next to Detective Agencies should give you a fair range of contacts. At the start, when versos and rectos blur and Times Roman and Century Bookman sound like historical periods rather than typefaces, face-to-face contact helps. Later you can do it by letter or on the phone. Ring round and ask if any have experience of bookwork and how much they might charge to help you. A first consultation should always be free. If in difficulty Keith James Design based at 39 Charles Street, Cardiff CF1 4EB (01222 222117) has helped many small and self-publishers and can be recommended.

The specialist self-publisher production house

If using a professional designer as the interface between you and your book appears too costly you could turn to one of the many specialists who offer help specifically for the self-publisher. The rise of these houses from virtually none a decade ago to at least a dozen operating in Britain today is a factor of increasing leisure and the booming sale of books. Ian Hilder at Antony Rowe Ltd believes that following the demise of the Net Book Agreement, under which prices were immutably fixed, mainstream publishers have become far more cautious about unknown authors. Self-publishing has become endemic with not every author, by any means, able to manage the complete process of production. The new houses offer help where many need it.

What can you expect? Anything and everything from a total deal where the author stays in cotton wool, completely absolved from the production process, to assistance on specific aspects such as origination or layout and design. Many have published their own pamphlets on how to self-publish and can usually quote case histories of authors they have worked for. Some own their own printing equipment and have developed their self-publishing specialism as a side line; others are more like design studios running desk-top publishing systems or reprographic bureaux using professional imagesetting machines.

Standards vary as wildly as the costs charged, and the advice offered, particularly when it comes to marketing and distribution, should be accepted with care. Check them out; ask for quotes. Read their literature. Contrast and compare. The costs will almost certainly be higher than those you would pay if you placed your work with a local printer. But hand-holding is what many of us need. How much is up to you.

The list which follows is not definitive, nor is it an indicator of recommendation: most are untried by the present author. Unlisted operators who would like to be included are invited to write in for possible inclusion in future editions of this book. The companies actually detailed offer a range of services and all appear to be free of the miasma of rip-off associated with the vanity press (see Chapter Three).

Alexander Associates, Howard Alexander, 4 South Street, Fowey, Cornwall PL23 1AR . Tel: 01726 832 900 Fax: 01726 833 900 e-mail: Alexander69@Delphi.Com

Axxent Ltd, John Cox, 99–101 St Leonard's Road, Windsor, Berkshire SL4 3BZ. Tel: 01753 857349.

The Book Press, John Downie, Unit H, Purdon Street, Partick, Glasgow G11 6AF. Tel: 0141 3399499 Fax: 0141 3371113.

Booksend and Book-in-Hand Ltd, Ann Kritzinger, 20 Shepherds Hill, London N6 5AH. Tel: 0181 341 7650.

Castle of Dreams, Alex Gerrard, 8 Pease Street, Darlington D11 4EU. Tel: 01325 381466.

Centreprint, Lanesfield Drive, Wolverhampton WV4 6UA. Tel: 01902 402693.

Evergreen Graphics, Cecil Smith, Meadow Lane, West Wittering, Chichester, West Sussex PO20 8LR. Tel/Fax: 01243 513395.

Ex-Libris Press Book Production, Roger Jones, 1 The Shambles, Bradford on Avon, Wiltshire BA15 1JS. Tel/Fax: 01225 863595.

Intype, Woodman Works, Dursford Road, Wimbledon, London SW19 8DR. Tel: 0181 947 7863.

Ipswich Book Company, Julie Walker, The Drift, Nacton Road, Ipswich, Suffolk IP3 9QR. Tel: 01473 711144 Fax: 01473 271412.

Manuscript Research (Printing Division), Val Miller, PO Box 33, Bicester, Oxfordshire OX6 7PP. Tel: 01869 323447 Fax: 01869 324096.

Pages, Susan Coon, Ballencrieff Cottage, Bathgate, West Lothian EH48 4LD. Tel/Fax: 01506 632728.

Penvar Books, Chris Pollard, Gerrans, Portscatho, Truro, Cornwall TR2 5DZ. Tel: 01872 580 914.

Prospero Books, Stewart Ferris, 46 West Street, Chichester PO19 1RP. Tel: 01243 771107 Fax: 01243 786300.

ProPrint, Riverside Cottage, Great North Road, Stibbington PE8 6LR.

Twm Publishing, Tim Moore and June Weller, 12 Horseshoe Park, Pangbourne, Berkshire RG8 7JW. Tel: 01734 844337 Fax: 01734 844339.

The short run salvation

Technology has come to the aid of self-publishers in more ways than simply speeding up and simplifying the process of origination. It has also come up with a printing method that is economic – well, relatively economic – on short runs. Based around photocopier technology – *xerography* – where a negatively charged powder toner is dusted on to a positively charged drum the system is clean, dry and simple. There are no plates to make and no liquids are used, although if you get loose toner over your shirt you'll certainly have to go home to change. As faster and faster photocopiers came on to the market – with some capable of printing both sides of the sheet and then dumping the sheets into a hopper system which would collate and staple the results – it was only a matter of time before someone designed the complete book-making machine. Text in one end; printed, bound books out the other. That machine is the Xerox DocuTech.

One of the first and most successful UK companies to install a DocuTech was short-run specialists Antony Rowe Ltd, (ARL), based at Bumper's Farm, Chippenham, Wiltshire SN14 6LH. (01249 659705 Fax: 01249 443103). ARL's existing specialisms in the field of journal printing, short-run work for niche publishers and facsimile reproduction of antiquarian books were expanded to include work for those interested in very short runs of new material. A short run is anything between 100 and 1,000 copies – ideal for the self-publisher.

ARL can accept material in any of the formats for camera-ready copy already discussed (or can actually format the material for you, for which there is an extra charge), or can run work directly from word-processed or desk-top published computer disks. The process by which ARL reads your disks and converts the material into printable pages is complex and assumes that your computer can output information in PostScript format. PostScript is a page description language which ensures text, headings, margins, etc. carry across as you intend them. The position of text on page and of one page relative to the next is critical. In this field PostScript is an industry standard. ARL produces a useful, if rather technical, set of *Digital Guidance Notes* which explain in some detail presentation procedures for both PC and Mac users.

DocuTech production has gone a considerable way to bring down the costs of limited production and can even output as few copies as one, although not many publishers are ever satisfied with a run that low. ARL DocuTech productions are stylish and of a high standard. They limit themselves to works of more than sixty-four pages and usually of less than 1,000 copies. Above this figure it is usual for conventional print to become a more cost-effective method of production. ARL works in this field too; ask for a quote.

The company is a *printer* and does not at present assist with sales or distribution (although there plans in the pipeline for an expansion in this area). They expect self-publishers to have a familiarity with book design. Send for their comprehensive price lists and descriptive brochures. Their charges are most competitive in the areas they specialise in – the short run. The more commercially minded self-publisher requiring a regular print run, or the unashamed pamphleteer, is advised to shop around.

13

DESKTOP PUBLISHING IS NO SUCH THING

Those of you who have read this far might be suspicious that desktop publishing, already mentioned quite a few times, might not be all it sounds. Others who might have turned directly to this chapter in the hope that it may offer them a simple desk-top route to actual books need to be disillusioned immediately. Desktop publishing is no such thing.

In printing nothing remains the same two months running. Such is the pace of change. Hard to believe that the first computer-set offset-litho produced book was published in Britain as recently as 1957. Centuries of movable type production demolished at one stroke, a whole panoply of industrial-sized setting machines swept away. Origination is now a digital process and that means setting on a screen.

DTP packages – the software which enables such setting to occur – are possibly the most misunderstood devices in the whole world of book production.

> These are called desktop publishing programmes, because, one assumes, they are run from the desk top and a publication results.
>
> Jane Dorner, *Writing On Disk*

I've known determined writers blow their entire savings on equipment which, once set up, has produced for them no more than a single unbound copy of the work they hold so dear.

What are they?

A DTP program will enable you, from your computer, to originate the pages of your book in a format usable by your printer. When all goes well such programs can save you a considerable amount of both time and money and keep you, there, in total control of how your book will turn out. Using DTP you can avoid physical paste-up completely. No adhesives to get over your trousers, no more ink on your finger-tips and no more swaying lines. DTP enables you to set text, to change face and point size at will, to word-wrap, to remove the rivers of white left by bad keying, to set headlines in differing faces, to arrange footnotes to perfection and to add, should you want them, a whole range of exquisitely formed lines, boxes, tints, shades, in-fills, text-reversals and shadows. Pages can be set so they mirror each other perfectly. The old problems of layout, the size and proportion of margins and the way the text sits between them can be solved at the click of a mouse. DTP can import text from files produced on a word-processing program or from typewritten text digitised by putting it on an optical character-reading scanner. Illustrations can be dropped in, manipulated, cropped, rotated, despeckled, changed in size and titled at will.

The idea is for you to produce the complete page-layout for your book efficiently and professionally, and for you to do it on your own. On screen you can check everything from choice of typeface to spelling before committing a thing. Nobody with a drawing pen ever got their rules and boxes as square and even as a DTP program. Perfection is available, so long as you know how.

Why not use a word processor?

Many contemporary word-processing programs such as Word, Ami-Pro and WordPerfect offer facilities similar to those available on fully blown DTP set-ups. Multiple faces, headlining, word-wrap, justification of text and a good many other features are now included as standard. For something not too ambitious this may well be all you need.

Where DTP programs score is in their ability to mix text and graphics. Word processors may offer limited clip-art (free, non-copyright images) and similar graphic facilities but they lack the flexibility and sophistication available under DTP. Nor are word processors likely to offer full page layout including printer's crop-marks (the places where the guillotine will cut) – essential if you intend going directly to plate – nor are they generally able to output their text in PostScript format – again an essential element if you intend avoiding literal paste-up. PostScript is a computer language used to describe page design in mathematical terms. It runs between computer and laser printer, converting what you see on screen into something the printer's output heads can handle. Its development in the early eighties was a landmark in computer setting.

Word processor output, usually to an ink-jet or laser printer at the relatively low resolution of 600 dots per inch, can be sufficient for many publications, as we have already seen. But to avoid the jagged look that this kind of output can give to the letter forms used (check an example with a magnifying glass to see what I mean) the higher resolutions available only via DTP to imagesetter are essential.

Common mistakes

Amateur page make-up, even after the benefits of expensive DTP, betrays itself in a number of ways. The most common is an unhappy combination of typeface or simply the mixing of too many. I've seen poetry books produced at community print shops where every headline uses a new face and the text swirls through a bewildering range of point sizes. Sometimes there is too much choice and when it is there, at the touch of a button, some operators go to town and use it all. Most professionals will limit themselves to no more than two faces in an entire book, often alternating a sans-serif face for titles with a serif face for the text itself.

Other frequent errors include the misuse of italic and bold type, blunders over spacing and carrying over the conventions of traditional typing by having things underlined. Page layout, as we have seen in the chapter on design, has a number of tried and tested rules. Learn them and then follow what they say. Design is as much about making the text readable as it is about looking great. DTP should give greater control but the rules governing how a page is to be set out are still the same.

What hardware do you need?

A computer. A PC or a Mac will be perfect, an Amstrad PCW or an Acorn BBC B most certainly won't. The bigger the hard disk, the larger the RAM, and the faster the processor the better. I would not expect much on anything less than a 486 with 8, or preferably 16 megs of RAM. If the machine has a CD drive then you will have ready access to a vast range of clip art and fonts and your software will not take too long to load. Go for a high-resolution screen, 15' or bigger. The larger the sceen the more of your page layout you will be able to see at any one time. Optional extras include a scanner to enable you to import illustrations, optical character recognition software to enable you to scan in text and, possibly, a modem, which would enable you to download your finished work via the phone line directly to your printer. Check the computer shops for prices and contrast and compare. If you know what you are doing you can take chances. Novices will need all the explanation and hand-holding they can get.

Which one?

As with most products there is a range available. At the cheaper end DTP can resemble a poor word processor with some added column manipulation. I've seen these products in game shop dumpbins for as little as £20. You'll get what you pay for. A professional DTP package – Ventura, QuarkXPress or PageMaker are the main ones – will set you back many hundreds of pounds but, in exchange, will do everything you need. But don't expect simply to spend the money, install the software and be ready to go. There is a very steep learning curve involved with DTP practice. Nothing is simple and good results will come only after you have spent a few months familiarising yourself with how the system works. Brian Cookman, who has written a very easy-to-follow DTP guide, *Desktop Design – Getting the Professional Look* (Blueprint), reckons that decent software on the beginner's computer is rather like a good target rifle in the hands of a novice. It may be perfectly designed for hitting the bull but that achievement will come only after quite a few tries. 'DTP is addictive,' he warns. 'Once you get the hang of handling it all, you will find you've missed your lunch because you were enjoying yourself.'

Training

If you are going to buy DTP then some kind of professional training is absolutely essential. Your capital investment on the hardware will be high and the price of sophisticated software will be similarly expensive. To do justice to the possibilities you now have at your fingertips you will need help. Training courses come in all shapes and sizes. Home study using a manual, exercise disks and perhaps an explanatory video will get you a decent overview. Month-long daytime courses for the professional will fit the bill but also completely empty your pocket. Part-time study by local authority evening class or at the community centre may be the answer. Before you embark be clear that what they are about to teach you will actually be of use. The lines between word processing and DTP have become blurred. A night class that explains how to cut and paste and format your paragraphs may be fun but it will certainly not be enough.

More technology

In terms of output technology already offers the self-publisher a fair number of alternatives to the printed hard-copy book and we'll be discussing these in Chapter Sixteen. But, for now, what else is available that might make the task of producing a traditionally styled self-published title just that little bit easier? The better-placed will already be using lap-top computers on which to prepare their text.

These briefcase computers with smaller screens can do anything their larger desk-top fellows can manage including running CDs and, if you want it, DTP. They enable work to be carried out anywhere – libraries, works canteens, trains. Take a spare battery with you – DTP packages zap up the power. Don't leave your lap-top on your seat along with your finished newspaper either. The lap-top that travels on alone to Crewe may not come back. And remember that the clickety-click of your fingers across the keyboard can annoy some people. A business acquaintance of mine was working on his company's spreadsheet on the five o'clock out of Paddington. He'd just got to the bit where the profit forecasts appeared to be falling into place when an old lady sitting opposite rapped the table hard with her umbrella. 'These trains are not for playing games on, you know,' she told him, 'and you a grown man. Put that toy away.' He did.

Light-pens and appropriate software which enable small amounts of text to be scanned and dumped directly into your database or even the pages of your book are a possibility. No need for note-taking or photocopying – they do your research in half the time. If you have a mobile phone and a suitable modem you can also engage in text transmission directly to the bureau from wherever you happen to be – beach, bar, park – but maybe not yet from a moving car.

In terms of software there are also available a number of aids to composition. Standard word processors will manage your spelling and your grammar but, if stuck, you can also buy programs which help with plot. There are rhyming dictionaries for poets, who-done-it plot manufacturers which offer you a constant stream of new directions as you write, even a poem generator which requires the user to do no more than depress a key. Fifty-thousand lines of random verse in a matter of seconds, and all by you.

Technology offers many possibilities and a host of solutions. Not yet the machine that can read for us – we could sleep nights then instead of wasting our time pouring over dusty volumes – but I'm sure Microsoft will have something out along those lines soon.

14

SELLING

To write books is easy, it requires only pen and ink and the ever-patient paper. To print books is a little more difficult, because genius so often rejoices in illegible handwriting. To read books is more difficult still, because of the tendency to go to sleep. But the most difficult task of all that mortal man can embark on is to sell a book.

From a poem by Felix Dahn paraphrased by Sir Stanley Unwin

You have the books in the house – finished at last. If your print run was wise, they'll fit under the bed or fill a wardrobe. If your enthusiasm got the better of you they'll block the hall, two tiers deep, and only thin people will be able to reach the lounge. Keep them packeted; resist the overwhelming desire to get them all out and handle them. Under wraps they stay clean and dust-free. The future is capricious – some of them may have to stay like this for years.

You are now faced with the hardest part of all. Considerably more difficult than seeing the book through the press, and monstrously more so than writing it. Selling is certainly no small thing that will look after itself. It is an energy-consuming operation with a legitimate claim to a large slab of any publisher's resources. If you do it well, you can found dynasties. America was built by the people who invented the sale of leather-bound books by the yard and promoted *Encyclopaedia Britannica* ownership as a status symbol for the non-English-speaking immigrant.

Selling is anathema to many writers; it is onerous and accomplished half-heartedly, if at all. If this is you then, as a self-publisher, you are in the most danger. Without some ability, your project will slide into vanity and fail. There is no philosopher's stone which, once discovered, will enable you to sell your book on DIY gun-running to the peace movement. But there are ways of improving your chances.

The first fact to face is that despite a high proportion of literate individuals in our population of over fifty-six million, few people actually read books. They manage newspapers and magazines; they read the text of television advertising; they consume huge quantities of junk mail – special offers for inflatable beach furniture printed up the side

of oven-chip bags and endless imperatives to buy posted on taxi
doors, bus windows, the backs of tickets and on the ends of books of
stamps. But literature – no; books – no. These are boring; it takes too
long to get to the end. In a dental waiting room recently I was the
only one with my head in a novel; everyone else stared out into
space. Try to buy a set of bookshelves in an average-sized town. There
are plenty of chipboard constructs good at displaying ceramic table-
lamps, hi-fi equipment and glass fish but proper, adjustable shelving
suitable for a solid wall of books seems to be no longer made. The
last set I got I had to construct myself.

Most self-publishers have little idea about selling. If you are not
sure of the difference between an invoice and a delivery note and have
only a vague idea of what kind of discount a bookshop will expect
then follow this chapter with care. As a self-publisher it will be a wise
move for you to find out.

What price should the book be?

There are two ways of deciding this, one based on what the market
will stand and the other on how much production actually costs.
Good pricing should really combine both.

Most people will pay only what they consider to be a fair price
for a book. This must be set at a level no higher than comparable books
of the same size, shape, production and on the same subject. Whatever
you produce, the market is always competitive. Your mountain guidebook priced at six times the going rate because it cost you that to get
all the photos included will not sell. Explanations as to how many
difficulties you faced and the level of your production costs will be
ignored. The customer is concerned solely with value as he or she per-
ceives it. If it is wrongly priced it will not go.

On the other hand, marketing titles at a pound when they cost two
will undoubtedly help shift them but won't get the money back.
Commercial publishers often begin with their unit costs multiplied
by five – roughly one for production, one for the author, one for profit
and two for distribution. Self-publishers have smaller overheads so
multiply by three: one for production, one and a half for distribution,
and a half for themselves.

Compare this price with the market price. Go round the bookshops
and check contemporary products and make adjustments to bring your
pricing into line. It is vital to get it right. You must cover not only
your complete production costs but your full distribution charges as
well – and some of these you have yet to incur.

Distribution costs can include the following:

- carriage on delivery of books
- packaging on delivery of books
- an overheads charge to cover promotional activities
- storage charges
- freelance representation commission (your own travelling costs if you do it yourself)
- professional distribution percentage
- stationery costs for the production, preparation and despatch of delivery notes, invoices and statements
- time – but lots of self-publishers give this for free.

Try to estimate these before you begin. Booksellers do not take kindly to carriage charges added to their invoices because you have forgotten to include that element in your price, nor to reduced discounts because that is the only way you can bring your prices into line with what you imagine the market will stand.

Do not print a price on your book but use removable stickers. If repricing is necessary then the customer will not feel cheated by finding an earlier and lower price underneath.

Sales basics

Commercial practice is not routinely taught at school – it ought to be. Payments by business organisations are rarely made gratuitously. As any accountant will tell you, extracting money requires a specific technique. The usual practice is for deliveries to be accompanied by a *delivery note*, followed later by a cross-referenced *invoice* which asks for payment and this subsequently summarised in a *statement*. A statement details all invoices issued and payments received in a specified preceding period. All documents quote both the purchaser's order number or reference and its date of issue.

To save time, the self-publisher may combine delivery note and invoice into one document. Preparation is entirely the publisher's responsibility. The document should contain the seller's name and address, buyer's name and address, a unique reference number, date of transaction, reference to the buyer's order number and its date, details of the books, their price, the discount offered and finally the amount due. If this is to be made payable to someone other than the named publisher – Ron Ellis rather than Nirvana Books for example – a note to this effect should be included. This *delivery note/invoice* should be left with the books at the time of their delivery.

95

Some businesses do not pay for each of their supplier's deliveries separately but wait for a monthly statement summarising transactions and pay then. To avoid the complexities of having to issue both an invoice and a statement mark your *delivery note/invoice*: 'No statements issued. Please pay on this invoice.'

If, after a period of thirty days, your invoice remains unpaid send at first a reminder in the form of a copy of the original invoice with the words 'First Reminder' marked on it in red. Recalcitrant payers need stronger action. You are the tiniest of suppliers and your threats to withhold future deliveries – the technique used by the big publishers – will have little effect. Ring up, be firm, refuse to be put off with the standard 'it's in the post' response. If all else fails, turn up in person and threaten to annexe goods of equivalent value in order to settle to debt.

Duplicate invoice pads can readily be bought from office supplies outlets and from general stationers.

Getting orders – selling to bookshops

The traditional place to sell books is a bookshop. Not all self-publishers find shops the best or even the most appropriate place from which to sell their wares. Richard Binns, whose classy guidebooks to Britain and France make obvious promotional gifts, has successfully sold them directly to 'drug, ferry, credit-card, villa rental and dozens of other types of company'. Climbing books, such as those from Harry Mulholland, sell better from mountain centres and outdoor equipment shops, while local histories need very wide distribution through every available outlet in the district concerned and will not succeed if ghettoised in a single shop.

Nonetheless, the bookshop is a good place to start and for the serious self-publisher represents a nut which has to be cracked.

There are two ways of interesting a bookseller in stocking your wares – repping in person and repping by phone. Both systems have their advantages and I shall deal with them in turn. Repping in person is the harder. 'Repping is tough – you ride on a smile and a shoeshine; you have to boast so modestly while the buyer sniffs the goods,' says self-publisher Robin Chapman.

Make a list of your prospects. Begin with the local ones where you have the huge advantage of being a 'local author' which invariably encourages better reception and larger potential sales. For a list of more than three thousand UK bookshops consult the BA's *Directory of Booksellers Association Members*, 154 Buckingham Palace Road, London SW1W 9TZ (0171 730 8214). Also useful is Peter Marcan's

SELLING

Outlets for Specialist New Books in the UK: a Subjective Classified, Descriptive Directory, Peter Marcan Publications, PO Box 3158, London SE1 4RA (0171 357 3158). The really keen will try Saur's *International Directory of Booksellers*, although owning a copy of this reference tome will set you back several hundred pounds.

Do not simply turn up but prepare the ground – ring up to make an appointment. Ask to see the buyer or the manager. Say you are from Nirvana Books, never admit to being Ron Ellis, the author. Phone in the morning or mid-afternoon. Avoid the bookselling peak times of the lunch hour and anytime on Saturday, especially the afternoon.

At the appointed hour, arrive bearing books and invoice pad. Be respectably dressed. Avoid smelling of garlic or beer. Explain that your title is the best and ultimate book by Ron Ellis, your author. Intimate that you have publicity in hand – leaflets, local newspaper coverage and, if you've managed it, an interview on radio or TV. Admit to offering full trade terms. The moment the buyer agrees to purchase, fill out the invoice, hand over the books (if you have enough with you) and leave. Do not stay talking – given half a chance to think, the buyer may decide on less.

The secret of good repping is to be knowledgeable, friendly, ruthlessly efficient and fast. No mumbling or Tesco carrier-bags full of your sandwiches. Don't rubbish your rivals – for the purposes of your sale they do not exist. Remember that the buyer is more interested in making money than helping you, although some will offer to buy a minimum of copies just to make you go away. If they ask for five say that half-a-dozen would be better. If twenty, then ask if they could manage two dozen; say the books are packeted in twenty-fours. Close the deal, smile and go.

Repping to shops outside your immediate area requires careful planning. Travelling costs are expensive and have inevitably to be incorporated into the price of the book. Big cities with a university and therefore a number of shops are usually worthwhile, as of course is central London. (For an amusing account of one self-publisher's adventures in this field see *Dante Alighieri's Publishing Company* by Eric Lane [Dedalus Press].) Make sure you have firm, agreed appointments before you set out to travel any distance. Be punctual. If you travel by car take stock with you for immediate order fulfilment – much better than having to send the books on.

Hitting the chains

The four largest bookselling chains in Britain, John Menzies, W. H.

Smith, Waterstone's and Dillons, all require special handling.

Menzies comment as follows: 'We are high street retailers of books and as such we select titles which we feel are suitable to our customers' requirements and are not in the academic or *very* literary markets.' To get your book taken by the whole chain an approach should be made to head office. A written submission enclosing a jacket and advance information on the title is preferred. If judged by central book buyers to be suitable expect to give Menzies between 50 per cent and 55 per cent discount *and*, after a period, take back unsolds. Books of more local interest (because of either their subject or their author) can be sold directly to the local branch. Ring the buyer and make your pitch. If you are taken expect to give a minimum of 40 per cent on full sale or return.

W. H. Smith now buy by market category and have a team of individual buyers handling sectors such as gardening, cookery, television and crime. Fiction is still fiction, although this does now include poetry. Like Menzies they prefer the written approach to head office and if the product is selected will buy huge quantities but will demand similarly enormous discounts and will expect everything to be on sale or return. Local interest items can still be repped directly to the nearest branch. Expect to end up offering at least 60 per cent discount with stock fully returnable.

Waterstone's, the chain which altered the face of British bookselling by offering *everything* in large, highly browsable premises, now form part of the W. H. Smith group and are supplied centrally from warehouses in Swindon. Nonetheless their buying is still a matter they control themselves. Central purchasing is not the way forward here. Self-publishers need to open an account with Waterstone's head office in Brentford and then approach the hundred or more branches individually. A branch directory is available. Expect to offer 45 per cent on hardbacks and 48 per cent on paper, fully sale or return.

Dillons, the second component of the British bookselling revolution, operate on a similar basis. The first step is the opening of a supplier account through head office at Solihull. Central purchase is possible, although the chain prefer to work in co-operation with publishers by sending details of appropriate books to their branches. Repping and order collection is then left to the publisher. A directory of branches is available on request. Expect to offer anything between 35 per cent and 55 per cent, depending on what the shops decide to buy.

In all cases the publisher will be expected to pay carriage on the deal and to pay for it in both directions.

John Menzies, Retail Division, Hanover Building, Rose Street, Edinburgh EH2 2YQ (Tel: 0131 225 8555).

W. H. Smith Ltd, Greenbridge Road, Swindon SN3 3LD (Tel: 01793 616161).

Waterstone's Booksellers, Capital Court, Capital Interchange Way, Brentford TW8 0EX (Tel: 0181 742 3800).

Dillons the Bookstore, Royal House, Prince's Gate, Homer Road, Solihull, West Midlands (Tel: 0121 703 8000).

Doing it on the phone

In technique, telephone repping is similar to repping in person. Ring at non-peak times and ask for the buyer. It is easy to make extravagant claims over the phone but don't overdo it. Be businesslike and never claim your books are something they are clearly not. It is fair enough, however, to avoid mentioning that you are really a self-published amateur. Over the phone there are no unprofessional invoices, non-rep briefcases or idiosyncratic book production to give the game away. Be as brief as you can. Accept the order, making sure you get an official order number or reference, and then move on to the next shop on your list.

Telephone selling gets you around the country quickly and cheaply which is a great advantage. If, however, you have a really attractive product then you should try to rep in person. Some books sell best when they are seen.

Discounts

The trade standard is 35 per cent, a sliver above a third off the published price, on two or more copies *with carriage paid by the publisher*. Orders for single copies are discounted at only 25 per cent and sometimes have carriage costs or a 'small order surcharge' levied on top.

The trade dislikes little orders; it thrives on bulk. Full terms, 35 per cent off or more if you let them squeeze it out of you, should be offered only under *firm sale* conditions. The shop buys and within thirty days pays your invoice. The question of whether or not you'll take any unsolds back at a later date is a matter for negotiation (although as we've seen the big chains appear to demand this facility as a matter of course). *See-safe* conditions need to be confirmed at the time of ordering. These are exactly the same as for *firm sale* except that you agree *in advance* either to swap any eventual unsolds for other books you may publish or failing that to buy them back. Do not encourage see-safe terms unless forced to.

A final variation is true *sale or return* – often confused with see-safe by the trade itself – and usually the only option open to publishers of poetry and creative literature. Here money does not change hands until after the books have been sold on to shop customers. The publisher leaves a suggested number of copies and returns a month or so later to collect unsolds or restock and at that point presents the shop with an invoice for any items which have gone. It is not a really satisfactory system from the point of view of the publisher, although perfect from the shop's, and I would recommend those forced into it to offer only 25 per cent discount no matter how many copies are eventually sold.

Distributors and freelance reps

It may be that your personal resources end with the book's production and that you cannot face or accommodate having to turn up each morning at a fresh bookshop in order to peddle your wares. In any event, this will work satisfactorily only if the title is non-specialist, unesoteric and basically saleable. The solution is to engage a representative to carry the book on your behalf. Freelances, people who will work on a commission-only basis, can regularly be found advertising their services in the columns of *The Bookseller*. Freelances are usually hunting for a list rather than a single title but it is always worth asking. If you can't find one, place a classified advertising your need. Expect a rep to demand between 10 per cent and 15 per cent on top of what you are already giving booksellers. Reps will tour their part of the country collecting orders. On a regular basis these will be transmitted to you for fulfilment.

A further possibility is to engage a professional distributor. A number of companies exist who will operate on behalf of small publishers. Again these will usually prefer to work with someone running a list but there are exceptions. Services range from simple warehousing (they store the books for you) and order fulfilment (they mail out books and invoice the customer) – to a complete service including representation, invoicing, cash collection, credit control and stock management. Costs range from 15 per cent of turnover for simple warehousing to 25 per cent for the full package.

Comprehensive listings of warehouse and distribution services in the UK are included in Cassell and The Publisher's Association

Directory of Publishing and Pira International's *The Book Distribution Handbook* (Michael Barnard and Ray Webb). Both can be ordered through booksellers. The following companies have also indicated a willingness to deal with self-publishers. If you are considering working this way do check exactly what the company is offering you and the rates they intend to charge. Watch out for fixed costs and the line to be taken over returns.

Gazelle Book Services Ltd, Falcon House, Queen Square, Lancaster LA1 1RN (Tel: 01524 68765 Fax: 01524 63232).

John Rule Sales Marketing, 40 Voltaire Road, London SW4 6DH. (Tel: 0171 498 0115 Fax: 0171 498 2245). *Art, architecture, crafts, leisure, body/mind/spirit/ and some fiction. No poetry. Makes a one off set-up charge.*

Melia Publishing Services, Terry Melia, PO Box 1639, Maidenhead, Berks SL6 6YZ (Tel: 02628 410537 Fax: 01628 789758).

Paul Green, 83(b) London Road, Peterborough, Cambs PE2 9BS. *Specialist poetry and avant-garde titles only.*

Roundhouse Publishing Group, Alan Goodworth, Director, PO Box 140, Oxford OX2 7FF (Tel: 01865 512682 Fax: 01865 559594). *Non-fiction only; no poetry, biography, children's, cookery or crafts.*

Shelwing Ltd, 127 Sandgate Road, Folkestone, Kent CT20 2BL (Tel: 01303 850501 Fax: 01303 850162).

Turnaround Publisher Services, Bill Godber, Unit 3, Olympia Trading Estate, Coburg Road, London N22 6TZ (Tel: 0181 829 3000 Fax: 0181 881 5088).

Vine House Distribution, Richard Squibb, Waldenbury, North Common, Chailey, East Sussex BN8 4DR (Tel: 01825 723398 Fax: 01825 724188).

Vale Packaging Ltd, Debbie Chapman, Managing Director, 420 Vale Road, Tonbridge, Kent TN9 1TD (Tel: 01732 359387 Fax: 01732 770620).

Welsh Books Centre/Canolfan Llyfrau Cymraeg, Stad Glanyrafon, Llanbadarn Fawr, Aberystwyth (Tel: 01970 4455). *Welsh language and Welsh interest publications only.*

These are just a few of the many such companies self-publishers might consider using. Write to them for further details.

Despatch

Even those self-publishers with a distributor will at some stage have to pack up a batch of books and send them through the post. Don't make a meal of this. The traditional Post Office-preferred method of packing a parcel can be inordinately time-consuming. A cardboard box with strengthened corners, wrapped in brown paper, criss-crossed with string, and all knots sealed with wax may get a tea pot safely through the mail but overdoes it a bit for books, even assuming you can get your hands on the wax. On the other hand, simply sellotaping them into a plain envelope will mean they arrive with spines cracked and corners bent. Damaged books are the responsibility of the sender. The aim is to make your packets impervious to rough handling and to do this as quickly and cheaply as you can.

Recycle everything – boxes, packing, padded bags, string. Use sticky labels to obliterate previous addresses. Cut cardboard boxes into sheets around two-and-a-half times the width of the books and one-and-a-half times as high. Fold these around the books so that the card projects by a few inches both top and bottom. Seal open edges with tape. If it is a fat packet, tie it round with string as well. The top and bottom edges should now appear wedge-shaped and will protect the books' corners from being hurt. No brown paper needed; certainly no newspaper padding which will get newsprint on to the pages. This is the professional way. Cheap and swift.

For larger shipments, you'll need to stack inside a pre-formed card-board box, layering the books in alternate directions. Fill all free space with screwed-up paper, card scraps or broken polystyrene waste. Pick up the box and shake it: the contents should not move. Can your books now be thrown across the room without damage? Carry out a field test to be sure.

Direct selling

So far, we've discussed using the book trade as the principal way of selling books. There are other methods. Commercial publishers may have discovered the efficacy of sales through non-bookshop outlets but have yet to move into selling directly to the public on any scale themselves. The *Oxford Book of Beans* can be had off the stand in the health-food shop although not yet directly from the publisher's head office in Walton Street. By common consent, publishers publish and booksellers sell. (Although things change fast – see Penguin's customer supply service Penguin Direct.) As a self-publisher, you do not yet figure in this interdependent scheme of things and can do what you like. Direct selling means that the bookseller's 35 per cent becomes yours – an interesting prospect. How effective you can be depends on what kind of salesperson you are and how specialist your product.

My own experience stems from many frustrating afternoons spent outside the central library trying to sell poetry books. The public are so accustomed to street flyer distribution that many automatically assume you are handing out things for free; you get insults from the uninterested; the grubby-handed always want to hold the product and unfailingly give it back; the whole process is worse in the rain – I used to sell about a copy an hour; the wino with the harmonica and the cardboard box would always do far better financially and he could hardly play.

Successful direct selling is possible if you are prepared to locate your audience. With poetry, this should clearly be a poetry reading. Stand at the back and sell copies as the audience arrive and leave. Guidebooks should have you outside railway stations and hawking at public events like marathon races, ideal home exhibitions, fairs, WI market days and jamborees. Sports books go outside the ground or in the clubhouse after a couple of beers – beware abuse. Local history has the broadest public of all and can be sold virtually anywhere people gather. If your title has this kind of broad appeal, knocking on doors may work. Take care: you are now in the realm of double-glazing salespeople, encyclopaedia reps and brush-and-broom vendors. Should you put your foot in the door? Read up on the techniques of selling to be sure.

Get it listed – copyright libraries

Intimately linked to selling is the providing of information on the book in order that potential buyers may know it exists. The two principal sources of book information in the UK are Whitaker's database of books in print and the *British National Bibliography* maintained by the British Library. For more information on these see Chapter Five. The appearance of your title in these two data sources is linked to your sending of copies, on publication, to the UK copyright libraries.

Under the Copyright Act 1911, publishers are under a legal obligation to deposit, within a month of publication, one copy of each title *free of charge* in the following places:

● The British Library, Legal Deposit Office, 2 Sheraton Street, London W1V 4BH.
● The Bodleian Library, Oxford.

- The Library of Cambridge University.
- The Library of Trinity College, Dublin.
- The National Library of Scotland.
- The National Library of Wales, Aberystwyth.

The British Library copies should be sent direct; the others in one packet, care of the Agent for the Libraries, Mr A. T. Smail, 100 Euston Street, London NW1 2HQ. Copies for the National Library of Wales need be sent only if specifically requested. Include no correspondence, and to the British Library merely a note indicating your selling price.

This free gift to the nation on your behalf has nothing to do with the establishing of author's copyright as discussed in Chapter Five. It has the altruistic purpose of providing publicly accessible depositories of everything in print. You can't refuse; if you fail to send copies then the libraries can take you to court.

The follow up

If you have been doing your own selling to shops, direct to the public and to friends (always ask them to buy; unproductive complimentaries are not a good idea) there will come a point when the initial wave of activity has passed its peak. Like painting the Forth bridge, you must now go back to the beginning, to the bookshops, and start again. Despite Eric Lane's axiom that 'a watched book never sells', you need to check. Don't show up after a week – you'll be disappointed. Leave it a month or more. Before announcing yourself take a good look around to see where they've hidden your title. If you find it, spine out on a top shelf, move it. When no one is looking place it, jacket forward, near the till or in the middle of the shop's main display. Self-publishers I've known restack directly on top of their rivals. If you can't see the book anywhere reintroduce yourself to the buyer – he or she will have forgotten you – and ask for a fresh order. Don't leave it to the shop to do this automatically as most won't.

A shop's reception to your books can be improved if you send in a few customers yourself. I've heard of poets clandestinely buying all their own books back via accomplices. This avoids the agony of the six pristine copies left one December returning, dog-eared and finger-marked, the following June.

If the book fails to sell then ultimately you'll have to face that fact. It is not necessarily that bad writing is to blame; it could well be the marketing. All does not have to be lost. Read on.

15

MARKETING AND PROMOTION

Books should be published, not just issued. We are not talking about salami.

Bill Adler

Selling and marketing are allied but they are not the same. The essence of selling is the disposal of the book you already have in stock. Marketing begins earlier. It involves research – finding out who your customers are, what they want and how you can provide that in the most economic form. Never publish blindly but temper the chance you take with hard information. Avoid vanity if you possibly can. If you are the main person the book is intended to please then you are liable to be its main customer as well.

Outline your market. What kind of people will be interested in what you intend to publish? How many of them are there? Where are they situated? What percentage will buy the book? The audience must be identified and targeted. Your publication must be geared to what they want, at a price they can afford.

For example, if you are publishing a guide and history to the local branch line you may expect your audience to consist of railway enthusiasts, historians and perhaps local people with a nostalgia for steam. In addition there will be an interest among model railway buffs and possibly former employees of the branch line itself. About how many of these people are there? That shouldn't be too hard to discover. How much will they be willing to pay? Is the district well off enough to support an expensive production, or should it be a pamphlet? What other similar books are available? How many of them are there and how will your book differ? What is their average price? The earlier you get this information the better.

Once the audience is identified, it must next be given the opportunity and encouragement to buy. 'It is no good assuming that the world is itching to buy your masterpiece,' as self-publisher Norman Hidden correctly remarked; 'almost certainly the world is not.' How will you convince your targeted audience that they want to buy a railway book and not just any railway book but yours? How will they buy it? Bookshops? Mail order? On the counter among the cabbages at the greengrocer's? This must all be planned in advance. Promotion without research and an incorrectly identified audience are a complete waste of time.

The campaign

The marketing campaign began with the title you chose, the design you put on the cover and the style and price at which you had it printed. These elements need to be decided with the target audience clearly in mind. Most authors correctly imagine that the best way to sell a book is to advertise it. Their mistake is to think that the best way to do this is by taking space in newspapers and magazines.

Space advertising is probably the least cost-effective form of promotion that a publisher may take. A few column inches in even the most local of newspapers can be expensive, the costs for the national dailies inordinately so. Adverts which do appear are usually placed by commercial publishers needing to please their authors. A space which costs £200, not untypical for an 800 x 1,200 block, will need to generate a considerable number of sales to pay for itself. The chances are that it won't. Do not be cajoled by sweet-sounding display advertising personnel who may ring you up and address you by your first name. Say no.

The best and most cost-effective form of advertising is actually free. Unlike any other industry, publishing receives huge media coverage in everything from the Sunday supplements to the local drive-home radio show absolutely gratis. All it costs to get yourself in line for benefit is a bit of planning. Your promotional campaign should run as follows:

Publication dates

Set a publication date. This is not the day on which you receive completed books from the printer but an artificial date fixed far enough in the future to allow you time to complete distribution to both shops and the media in advance. Pick a weekday; *OUP* publish on a Thursday and they are big enough and long established enough to know.

It is still accepted practice for booksellers not to offer titles for sale to the public until publication date (although there are a few signs that the convention is cracking). This practice prevents the large shops with an early shipped order for fifty from stealing a march over the independent specialist with a late-arriving subscription for three. Make sure that your booksellers understand that you want them to stick to the date you have set. It is also the intention that reviews should not be published before the official date. Customers hunting the shops for books which have yet to arrive are not a good idea. There are backsliders and slip-ups in both areas.

The worst mistake you can make is to set a publication date too early. I have attended at least two embarrassed publishers' launch parties where the books were only available in mock-up and one where the author had to give a recitation from memory, nothing else being to hand.

Flyers

Print a flyer: a small handbill announcing the title, author, extent, ISBN, publisher's name and address, publication date and price. Describe the work by reprinting the blurb. Promotional non-attributed quotations such as 'An exciting new collection from leading Liverpool poet Ron Ellis' or 'The most comprehensive history of the district yet published' will substitute for real ones. Try to incorporate a facsimile of the cover somewhere. An easy way is to have extra copies of the jacket or cover run on plain paper and the flyer details printed on the reverse.

Produce two versions: a trade flyer which includes information on discounts offered (see Chapter Fourteen); and a direct-sales version which incorporates a tear-off slip. It is best not to remind the trade that you are engaging in direct selling nor to inform the public of the level of discount you extend to shops. Remember to include a postage-and-packing charge on the direct sales version.

Flyers should be put in all outgoing mail (including the gas bill) as well as being sent directly to individuals, societies and institutions who you think may be interested in buying copies. A mailing list of addresses can be built up from the telephone book, the subscription lists of local societies if you can get access to them, editions of *Who's Who* and other directories. Much depends on the kind of book you are publishing. Spend a day at the reference library; to prepare a list big enough to be of use will take that long.

Trade flyers should be sent to bookshops you cannot reach on a personal visit. In addition, those shops should be mailed a copy of the book's cover in its laminated version. Remember to have extra printed and follow up with a telephone call (see Chapter Fourteen).

Try exchanging with fellow self-publishers – include one of their leaflets in each of your books while they include yours in theirs. Keen self-publishers leave flyers in library books and on the seats of buses. Ready-prepared mailing lists can be purchased: see advertisements in *The Bookseller*. Charges are high but it is cost-effective if your book is specialist enough (or desirable enough) to have a clearly identifiable audience. It is worth mailing a flyer on a book about dentistry to all UK dentists, for example.

Keep a bunch of flyers on your person and try to remember to leave copies lying around or pinned to notice boards wherever you go.

Press releases

Prepare a press release. Fear not, you are a writer: of course you can do it. The press release should contain the basic information on the book – title, publication date, price, etc. – together with some items of information about the content, the author or the circumstances of publication on which the receiving journalist may hang a story. Newspapers are not interested in creativity, writing ability or art. Telling them your short stories are first-class and previously published in *Stand* will result in nothing. If, however, you had to sell your best suit or resort to singing in the street in order to raise the cash for their publication or one of them is about how you were inadvertently rude to a member of the royal family then a few column inches may be assured. Put in anything of interest you can think of but expect journalists to cross-question you and for the story to come out completely differently from the way you intended.

Give the press release a title – 'Street Singer Turns Publisher', 'Defiant Local Author Explains Why He and the Palace do not Get On' or whatever. Include a contact telephone number and send the finished document to all the newspapers, radio and TV stations and magazines you can think of.

Be specific – direct your mail at named programmes, journalists or columns. The press release sent simply to the BBC or the local paper generally fails to arrive on the best desk. If you do not know who the most appropriate person is then ring up and ask. For further information see David Northmore's *How to Get Publicity for Free – How to Write a Press Release, Contact the Media, Gain Radio and Television Interviews, and Organise Press Conferences* (Bloomsbury) and Terry Prone's *Just A Few Words – On Everything You Need to Know if You Give a Lecture, Make a Speech, Appear on Television, be Interviewed on Radio or Comment at a Meeting* (Poolbeg).

In addition to talking to newspapers, you should also be prepared to speak on radio. Sometimes this involves sitting in a cramped studio in one part of the country being interviewed by someone you can't see and can hardly hear in a studio somewhere else. Usually it means turning up at 6.30 a.m. for a three-minute chat on the drive-to-work programme. Such exercises are always worth the effort. If invited, try not to plan what you are going to say in advance. Turn up and talk

– spontaneity makes better radio. Don't worry about stumbling. Your interviewer will take care of you, filling in any silences with rolling chat. If it's the BBC in any of its many guises always ask about a fee – they are often payable. With the independents you usually have to be thankful for the free airtime.

If you are criticised try not to be offended. All publicity is good publicity.

Review copies

Mail out review copies well in advance of the publication date. Include with each a printed slip announcing the book's title, author, publisher's name and address, price and a note to the effect that 'This book is sent for the favour of a review. Publication date: 18 June 1998, before which day no publicity or comment should appear. A cutting of any review or mention would be appreciated.'

There are two views on review copies. One is that they are just another freebie to be taken home by anyone on the newspaper who fancies them and then as often as not sold quickly on the second-hand market by poor journalists who need the money more than you. The other is that even if it takes thirty free copies to elicit one review then it is worth it.

Don't stint on review copies. Within reasonable limits send out as many as you can. Send to all the places on radio, TV and the newspapers which review similar publications. Follow the rules of the press release and send to named journalists or programmes, if you can. Link the review copy to the press release either by sending the two together or by mentioning in the release that review copies can be had on application. And don't worry about the cost – it may say £7.50 on the jacket but that is not what it costs you.

Follow up your despatch of gratuitous gifts to the critics with a phone call a few days later. Concentrate efforts on the best prospects – usually radio chat-shows and local papers. Draw attention to yourself. Inevitably you will be told that your review copy has not arrived. Do not be daunted. Take the person's name and send another. Nothing will happen unless you make it happen. As we've heard, Ezra Pound considered writing his own reviews – with do-it-yourself publishing it is not unheard of for that to actually happen.

Presentation copies

... a copy of a book which does not sell sent to you by the author.
Charles Lamb

Not a good idea, unless for the purposes of advertising you wish to get a quote out of someone. Send out flyers instead.

Launches

These are costly but can be worth it if they attract attention – much depends on the book's subject and intended audience. Poetry books can do well if launched with some free wine at the local bookshop and accompanied by a reading; a guidebook might rate a local society dinner; children's books can be celebrated by a fancy-dress story-telling complete with free balloons and badges at a toy shop. Whatever you do incorporate details in your press release. Don't just be active, be seen to be active. Get whatever coverage you can.

Listings

Get yourself listed everywhere. The book trade and library bibliographies have already been covered. Where appropriate, it is additionally worth writing to the following and requesting that information on your title or yourself as a publisher be included in their next edition. If you think there is a possibility of additional coverage, in the periodicals for example, enclose a press release.

The Directory of Book Publishers, Distributors and Wholesalers (an annual) published by the Booksellers Association, 154 Buckingham Palace Road, London SW1W 9TZ.

Directory of Publishing: UK, Commonwealth and Overseas, Cassell plc, Stanley House, 3 Fleets Lane, Poole, Dorset BH15 3AJ.

Writers' & Artists' Yearbook, A. & C. Black, 35 Bedford Row, London WC1R 4JH.

The Writer's Handbook, edited by Barry Turner, Macmillan, 25 Eccleston Place, London SW1W 9NF.

Whitaker's Directory of Publishing, J Whitaker & Sons, 12 Dyott Street, London WC1A 1DF.

Small Presses and Little Magazines in the UK And Ireland: an Address List, Oriel, The Friary, Cardiff CF1 4AA.

The Bowker Library and Booktrade Almanac, Bowker-Saur, Maypole House, Maypole Road, East Grinstead, West Sussex RH19 1HU.

Directory of Publishing in Scotland, Scottish Publishers Association,

Scottish Book Centre, Fountainbridge Library, 137 Dundee Street, Edinburgh EH11 1BG.

For poetry publishers:

Directory of Poetry Publishers and International Directory of Little Magazines and Small Presses, Dustbooks, PO Box 100, Paradise, Ca 95969, USA.

Poets Market, edited by Christine Martin, Writer's Digest Books, 1507 Dana Avenue, Cincinnati, Ohio 45207, USA.

Periodicals:

The Author, Journal of the Society of Authors, 84 Drayton Gardens, London SW10 9SB.

Books, 43 Museum Street, London WC1A 1LY.

Books For Keeps, children's book review magazine, 6 Brightfield Road, Lee, London SE12 8QF.

Books in Scotland, The Ramsay Head Press, 15 Gloucester Place, Edinburgh EH3 6EE.

Books Ireland, 11 Newgrove Avenue, Sandymount, Dublin 4, Ireland.

The Bookseller, journal of the book trade, J Whitaker & Sons Ltd, 12 Dyott Street, London WC1A 1DF.

European Bookseller, 15 Micawber Street, London N1 7TB.

LA Record, Journal of the Library Association, 7 Ridgmount Street, London WC1E 7AE.

Llais Llyfrau / Books in Wales, Welsh Books Council, Castell Brychan, Aberystwyth SY23 2JB.

Logos, 5 Beechwood Drive, Marlow, Buckinghamshire SL7 2DH.

Poetry and Little Press Information (PALPI), Journal of the Association of Little Presses, Stan Trevor, Briagha, Badninish, Dornoch, Sutherland IV25 3JB.

Publishing News, 43 Museum Street, London WC1A 1LY.

Writer's Monthly, Ashley House, 235/9 High Road, Wood Green, London N22 4HF.

Writers News, PO Box 4, Nairn, IV12 4HU.

If you have handled all this correctly you will by now have been the recipient of a decent amount of coverage. Successful promotion moves hand in hand with selling – if you are generating interest in your book, the shops will buy more. Make sure you tell them of the coverage you have had. At the same time, if people hear of your book they will also need to be able to buy it. Publicity which leads a customer into the bookshops before you have distributed copies is not a bit of good. Ten to one they will be told that the book does not exist and that will be the end of that. Public interest in anything is short-lived. When publicity comes, make certain that you are in a position to take advantage of it.

Hype

The things which benefit best from publicity are usually those which are already doing well. A basically poor book will rarely pay back heavy promotion. If you've followed the steps outlined in this chapter and your book is still not moving as fast as a tortoise in winter then the best thing to do might be to forget it and start again with something else. On the other hand, if sales are coming thick and fast then it might be worth trying to put them into overdrive with a little hype.

Success breeds success. Ring up the papers and tell them you are winning. They may run a story. Promotional gimmicks of the kind used by the big companies are usually beyond the pockets of self-publishers. You can't take the head of broadcasting on holiday or race a boat with your name on it across the Atlantic. However, you might take a few people for a drink if you are bold enough. You can suggest to a local bookshop that they hold a literary luncheon with you as guest or have you in one Saturday morning for a signing session. Local societies are always looking for speakers – ring up and volunteer. Will the building society devote a window to your book? Get an interview with the branch manager and ask. If it's the right title will the brewery sell copies through their houses? If you get any good publicity make photocopies and recirculate them. Keep telling people that what you are doing works.

Richard Binns reckons that staying in recognised channels is the path to ultimate failure for the self-publisher. His travel guides to France have all benefited from the Binns forthright approach. He begins by swamping travel journalists with review copies, sending out over 250, and following up with a campaign of phone calls. His object is to convince journalists that there is a feature story in the project. He has so far succeeded in getting coverage in four Sunday papers, two of them as illustrated features in the colour magazine. Once publicity is assured, Binns moves into sales. First he sells the foreign rights to an American publisher and anyone else interested, and then wholesales copies of the British edition as promotional gifts for use by travel firms, credit-card companies and hotels. Without publicity, the large orders would elude him. He has a wonderful product and he keeps telling people so.

Centaur Press's Jon Wynne-Tyson, an old hand at self-publishing, brought out a novel called *So Say Banana Bird* under his own Pythia Books imprint. In something of a publicity coup, the *Sunday Express* was convinced that Wynne-Tyson was, of all things, the King of Redonna, a tiny Caribbean islet. The novel, a tale of boats and bad doings, is by coincidence also set on an island in the Caribbean. Wynne-Tyson got four colour pages, photographs of himself erecting Redonna's flag (made from M. & S. pyjamas) and naturally a few heavy mentions of the book. The feature led to further media interest, including national radio, and achieved what Wynne-Tyson was after in the first place – sales of the book. If you have contacts, as Wynne-Tyson clearly did, then now is the time to use them. Promotion is not for the faint-hearted.

Ken Warpole, author of *Reading By Numbers* (Comedia), reckons that the top best-selling books as listed by the trade magazines represent not so much the books people want to read but those they are able to buy. The two are not the same. Promotion is convincing the public they want your book. Marketing is ensuring they get it. Unauthorly though these things may appear, as a publisher you are obliged to take them on.

16

IT DOESN'T HAVE TO BE A BOOK

There are many other ways of publishing yourself. One of the best is to do it in the company of others in a periodical, the historical alternative – *a little magazine*. Non-commercial periodicals have long been the outlet for minorities. Since the Pre-Raphaelites brought out the first indisputable little magazine in 1850, *The Germ*, groups of individuals without a platform have chosen the self-published magazine as the way to get on.

> let's start a magazine
> to hell with literature
> we want something redblooded
>
> e.e. cummings

Today there are well over 250 literary little magazines in Britain, along with countless amateur fanzines covering ray guns, ghouls, vampires, indie music, comics, football, skateboarding, ufology, junk food and ways to dye your hair. There are local history journals, parish magazines, association newsletters, bridge club newsheets, film fanatics' forums plus a vast range of listings magazines covering what's on. Most arise from the impetus of a single individual and many turn out to be a major outlet for that person's work.

Magazines avoid the stigma of vanity attached to self-publishing as the editor's work appears alongside that of others. There is an illusion of publication achieved through competition and less odium of ego.

The magazine I edited, *Second Aeon*, was begun mainly as a vehicle to get myself into print. It ran through the late sixties and early seventies, achieved a high circulation and became one of the main outlets for the poetry of the day. Yet the first issue – 100 copies, run-off on an office duplicator – was 80 per cent work by me. Miserable stuff too, looking back at it. Angst without humour but at the time I thought it showed real insight. During this period I worked for a local authority and on the day of publication spent the lunch-hour standing outside the canteen selling magazines for the price of a bag of crisps. By the time they'd finished serving the main course the whole print run had gone.

Magazine publication methods differ from those for books only in that you can get away with less. Four pages really fails to make it as a volume and yet is perfectly acceptable as Issue One of *Slugs on Mars*. Because of the variety of their content, magazines tend to be of larger format than books although with a lesser number of pages. There is an air of the disposable about them; books are for keeps.

At the outset content may pose a problem. Obviously you cannot be seen to write everything yourself. If utterly lacking in co-conspirators, use pseudonyms. For fiction and poetry, contact the local creative writer's group who will no doubt deluge you with material. Your regional arts board (see Chapter Five) will be able to give you more guidance on who the local writers are and where they meet.

As things progress, contributions will most likely become the least of your worries – there are now far more people writing than there are outlets. Exchange copies of your periodical for those of others. Run a page of reviews and comment. If you publish poetry, await the flood. Even the least known and recondite of small poetry journals can expect to trawl at least forty new pieces of verse a week.

Try to edit on your own. Joint decision-making or selection of content by committee can seriously weaken any taste or flair for editing that you may have. In my experience the benign dictatorship is far preferable to the bland selection panel. Go with your taste; make a mark.

Magazines are easier to sell than books. Motivate your contributors to help and offer them a discount. Street-selling is less personal with periodicals and therefore easier to manage. A refusal to buy is a rejection of the magazine rather than yourself. Run a subscription list. Demand that potential contributors buy the magazine first. As a slimmer product, the magazine will have a lower price and buyers will be easier to get. Magazines are less specific and if you are good at polite pestering many people will buy a copy just to make you go away.

Finance is easier too. As a periodical rather than a one-shot book, you can far more readily sell advertising space. This is best done by concentrating effort on known advertisers. If companies have bought space once they may well do so again. Research publications similar to your own and make a list of potential prospects. Ring at non-peak times and ask if they'd like to place some copy. Don't mention how you came across their name. Let them assume that it is their company image which caused you to call. If you can find the name of their advertising or promotions manager use it. If you can call strangers by their first names and sound convincing this helps – you'll sell more space.

What to charge? As a rule of thumb, double whatever the space cost you to produce. Ring up similar magazines and find out what they charge; pose as an advertiser and ask them to send you their rate card. In many cases, companies buy space as a form of sponsorship

– encourage this. Try to sell full pages rather than halves; reserve for special targets your outside back cover at four times the regular rate; charge extra for colour or for having to carry out the design and setting yourself; and if you are provided with camera-ready copy by the advertiser then remember to send it back.

You'll need to invoice your advertisers in order to gain payment. This is usually done after publication and should be accompanied by a cutting of the advert or a copy of the magazine itself.

Grants are a real possibility with magazines, especially those with literary or artistic aims. Many Regional Arts Boards have funds specifically allocated for this purpose. Conditions vary from area to area but invariably applications must be made in advance. If you are considering starting a mag then write in now.

ISBNs do not apply to magazines and listings are not included in Whitaker's database. However, *International Standard Serial Numbers* – ISSNs – are allocated to all magazines by the ISSN UK Centre at The British Library, Boston Spa, Wetherby, West Yorkshire LS23 7BQ (01937 546 959). If you'd like to know more then ask for their leaflet. The free deposit conditions of the Copyright Act 1911 also apply, (see Chapter Five).

For more information on journal production it is worth checking out Graham Jones's simple yet comprehensive introduction to the subject, *How to Publish a Newsletter* (How To Books), or Alan Greene's *Publishing Your Own Specialist Magazine* (Kogan Page).

Magazines are many times more exciting than books: you meet more people and you run more risks. The self gets smothered and this is the danger. Authors who turn editor can end up doing no writing of their own at all.

Beyond the book

Printed books are finished. So people have been saying since at least the sixties and yet books are still with us. Are any of the alternatives really viable? Depends on what you are trying to do. Telephone answering machines are a current fashion. They are mass produced, cheap, easy to plug in. Instead of an identifying outgoing message, people put on jokes, sound effects and poems. The caller has to listen to your haiku about halitosis or a three-minute ghost story before they are allowed to leave a message. This used to be called dial-a-poem when the Welsh Arts Council pioneered it in the UK during the seventies. Today innovative amateurs use the machine to carry their novels. Very brief chapters, changed once a week.

Serial publication on postcard is another possibility. Mail Art has authors and artists sending each other sequences of cards. The message is not complete until you have received each one. Poet Stewart Brown published a number of pieces of his work on postcards and distributed them free and rather surreptitiously via the racks at the Tate Gallery shop. Visitors liked what they found but when they tried to buy, Brown's ruse was uncovered, the cards removed and the poet banned.

An Arts Council of England study into the market for poetry recently suggested that the way forward for verse may not be with the book at all but rather with the single poem. The success of Judith Chernaik's Poetry on the Underground scheme where individual poems by poets past and present ride the tubes seems to prove the point. Posters reach a mass audience never penetrated by time-consuming books. Easy to print, nice to own but difficult to distribute and certainly, other than hand to hand, hard to sell. But there are self-publishers, poets and even short fictioneers, who have tried.

Talking books – literature on audio cassette – has been one of the great growth industries this decade. Household ownership of cassette players in all their many guises has now risen to 80 per cent. Listening to books while on the move or engaged in some other activity is clearly a thing people like to do. The ubiquitous double-cassette pack recording of Thomas Hardy, Charles Dickens or Jeffrey Archer has moved writing into yet another sector of the market where consumers lack the time to read printed books. Current UK output is above 10,000 different titles. For self-publishers it is perhaps the easiest book alternative to explore. Poets who are good performers will find it an obvious medium. It is suitable for lectures, essays, short stories, self-help and how-to works along with novel extracts. Anything that can be written can be read. Illustrate with sound effects, add music and think of it as repeatable radio.

You do not need much to make a cassette. It needn't be recorded in a studio – domestic equipment will often do. The machines most of your audience will use for play-back will be pretty basic. Unlike print where unit costs reduce the more you run, each fresh cassette costs the same. Reproduction at home can be achieved using twin-deck machines. For better quality employ a local cassette duplication company – details in *Yellow Pages*. If your area doesn't list a suitable firm then try the classified advertisements in the music press. Covers and labels can either be conventionally printed or photocopied. Colour sleeves produced by copier can really make a mark.

There are a number of shops now specialising in talking books (The Talking Bookshop in London and Books On Tape in Brighton). The range of titles available can be checked in *The Spoken Word Catalogue* published by Retail Entertainment Data. The annual *Writer's Handbook* lists audio publishers. If completely lost contact The Talking Tape Company at 5 Royal Crescent, Cheltenham GL51 9NH (01242 257200) who in addition to publishing their own titles act as audio consultants and audio cassette duplicators.

Fax-on-demand is a form of publishing much underrated, in the UK at least. Here data (information, fiction, poetry, whatever) is stored on a machine linked to the phone line. A caller reaching your fax-back number is greeted with your digitally recorded voice offering them a menu and asking them to key the code for the items they want into their phone key-pads. A whirl and the item rolls from the caller's fax machine, just like that. Swift, sure, slick and available twenty-four hours a day. The downside is that both you and your reader need to own fax machines and any money to be made on the transaction goes directly to the company providing the phone line. Nonetheless the system is a good way of issuing updates to existing publications or disseminating information about new products. In the United States Para Publishing's Dan Poynter, a self-publishing guru of long standing, has an impressive bank of interesting data available on his fax number. Call 001 805 968 8947 and you could soon be in possession of a mass of topical information on marketing, promotion and production for self-publishers. Request item 874 for a complete two-page report on the fax-back system itself. Para Publishing – who can also provide this material in hard copy form by post – is at PO Box 2206, Santa Barbara, California 93118-2206, USA.

Electronic publishing

In the early eighties the editor of *The Times* assembled his reporters to warn them of the forthcoming demise of the printed word. 'Imagine sitting on a train, pressing a button on your watch and receiving the latest news and opinions available, there and then,' he told them. 'Who would buy a paper?' But nearly twenty years on newspapers are as popular as ever. 'What kind of fool is going to sit on a train pressing a button on his watch when he can flick through his newspaper at will, do the crossword, doodle in the margin and swot the occasional 8.30 Reigate to Victoria bluebottle with the thing when required?' says writer David Hewson.

Despite this electronic publishing is here and rising. You may not yet be able to read its products in the bath but it is nonetheless a considerable force to be reckoned with. The book trade is suspicious of *multimedia* (the grab-all phrase used to cover electronic publishing's many directions) because it has its roots not with traditional book publishers but with the manufacturers of computer software. This is writing bounced in from somewhere else. 'The companies most prominently involved in electronic publishing rejoice in the deeply non-book-related names of Microsoft and SoftKey,' notes Andrew Rosenheim, formerly electronic publishing director at OUP. Many bookstore outlets do not know how to handle the product. They either lack the hardware to run demonstrations or don't have staff with enough knowledge to answer customer's questions. Too often the book trade imagines electronic products to be the province of the music store or the out-of-town computer supermarket. Maybe it will all soon go away, they hope. Believe me, it won't.

At its simplest publishing this way is merely a matter of making your work available on computer floppy disk. With some neat manipulation of text, clip-art import and a zippy colour headline (as available on nearly all contemporary main-line word processing packages) the disk can be copied on the home PC and sold on demand. Already small and self-publishers are taking advantage of this. Michael Blackburn at *Sunk Island Review* produces poetry books, issues of his magazine and descriptive catalogues this way. Write to him at PO Box 74, Lincoln LN1 1QC to see what can be done.

The format may appear ideal for frustrated novelists daunted by the costs involved in producing a hard-copy edition of their work themselves. A disk or two plus a smart wrapper and the thing is published – available in the big wide world. But there are problems. Not everyone yet owns a PC, and a good many people are never likely to. In any event reading text from a flickering monitor is hardly the best way to absorb fiction. 'The discomfort of reading large blocks of text on screen is notorious,' says Rosenheim, 'although the causes of this – poor screen displays and a lack of portability in small computers – are slowly being eroded.' Maybe the next generation, raised through school reading text from electronic monitors, will find things less difficult.

CD-ROM electronic publication – true multimedia – involves the use of huge resources and is undoubtedly beyond the self-publisher. Disks which can contain up to 125,000 pages of text plus a bewildering battery of sound, video and visual clips need heavy finance to create. Microsoft's all-singing all-dancing encyclopaedia, *Encarta*, and the children's titles from Dorling Kindersley are market leaders. Get a demo at your local computer superstore if you have never seen them and be prepared to be amazed. The medium is ideal for reference works and it already looks as if the future for specialist titles will go entirely this way.

Internet

The Net or Internet, is where change is at its fastest. Ten years ago unheard of and now within the reach of anyone with access to a suitable PC and the right software, the Net is a clamouring bedlam where individuals and corporations mix in a scramble for the future. Its propensity for change makes writing about it particularly difficult. As soon as one innovation is identified as the way ahead someone will come along with something better. Five years ago we all imagined that distant, text-only bulletin boards where we could leave examples of our writings for the perusal of fellow subscribers could be how publishing might go. Now we can all run our own animated, full-colour *home pages* stuffed to the gills with whatever we like and for very little cost.

The Internet is a complex worldwide web of interconnected computers. My desk-top PC gets connected through my phone line to anywhere I want in the world and all at the cost of a local call. Connection is perhaps not quite the right word here – if aficionados will permit a digression – you don't actually *connect* directly all the way to the Poetry Society or the Library of Congress, the Wrexham Weather Service or wherever it is you are trying to go. You reach them. Connections route via your *provider*, the company which makes the connection for you and charges you a monthly rent to log on to its giant computer. Sounds complex? Join in and it will all become clear. To take part you'll need at least a decent PC (or Mac), a phone line, a fast modem and appropriate software. This last item is currently free. Monthly subscriptions to a service provider can be had for as little as £5.00. Check out the specialist magazines: your local newsagent ought to be full of them.

The World Wide Web (WWW for short) part of the Internet allows its fifty million or so participants to interconnect via a series of screens full of information, known as pages. These pages can contain all kinds of data: statistics, jokes, displays selling holidays, sport's fixtures, weather maps, political invective, fan adulation, pop music lyrics, descriptions of space shuttle re-entry heat shields, information on hospital waiting lists, road condition reports. Anything and everything. Take a look – it'll be there. They can also contain creative work. If you hunt far enough you will find everything from the complete texts of many nineteenth century novels to a screen shot of Seamus Heaney, an example of one of his poems and, if you have the right equipment, his voice declaiming it right out of your computer's speakers. Users can read the information on screen, store it on disk, manipulate it if they wish to or print it out in hard-copy form on their printers.

Pages are connected via *hyper text links* which, when highlighted, take the user from one site to another. Thus the Society of Authors' page has direct links to (among many other useful places) the British Library, the Library of Congress, CNN Interactive News Service, the Internet Bookshop and Poetry London Newsletter. A browsing user of the Internet (a *surfer*) can waste a whole lifetime skipping from one site to another. The clever plan in advance where they want to go.

Dotted around the web are an increasing number of magazines (e-zines) which carry all kinds of content. To contribute you either add your material by keying it directly on to the site or forward your contributions by e-mail for the editor's perusal. Many writers have also discovered the joys of running their own sites (the aforementioned *home pages*). Space on the web is cheap and some providers offer it as part of their regular subscriptions. Self-publishing takes on a whole new set of clothes here. You are not publishing yourself on the Net because you have no other option but because everyone does it. Many writers see the Net as a platform from which to advertise themselves, their work and their books. Check out author Jane Dorner's page to see what can be done. Here Dorner has established an inter-linked set of pages which list her specialisms (writer, editor, speaker and craftsperson), her published books (which you can buy directly from her), information about her interests along with actual examples of what she has done. Within the first six weeks of running the site had attracted 267 visitors. Some of these visitors were friends but most she can't account for. Jane Dorner is at http://dspace.dial.pipex.com/jane.dorner/. Take a look then imitate. I have my own page at http://dspace.dial.pipx.com/peter.finch/ which is also worth a look. Why not post your entire collected poetry or your natural history of the sea slug on to the Net? With fifty million potential readers (and rising) it is an obvious area for development.

At the Author-Publisher Network, the self-publishers' self-help group (see Appendix One) Trevor Lockwood is convinced that in time the Internet will revolutionise the way individuals get themselves published. Not only will works make their first (and no doubt often their only) appearance on the Net but sales and marketing will also happen along this route. 'The change in technology allows authors to take control,' Lockwood insists. So long as authors can find a way of ultimately getting paid for what they mail off into cyberspace then all should be well. Watch this space, as they say.

If these developments interest you check out one of the many cyber-cafés open in most big towns. Here, for as little as £5 an hour, you can get a taste of the Internet and its participants while drinking your tea. Advice will be available in abundance. If the idea seems workable then get hooked up. Manipulating the computer languages needed to write a home page, HTML and Java, is a whole new ball game. But help for the beginner is readily at hand. Some specialist books on the subject are listed in Appendix Two.

17

POETRY: A SPECIAL CASE

All definitions get blurred when it comes to poetry, even over what precisely the stuff is. Tony Curtis, Professor of Poetry at the University of Glamorgan, suggests that for every rule set up to define it there will be an honourable exception. He concludes that in the end a poem is a poem because its creator calls it one. That's as fair a definition as I have ever come across. Poetry is the largest creative-writing participation sport we have going in this country. Almost everyone seems to have it in them, or imagines they have. Poetry is such an easy thing to manage. Bash off one after lunch or in that brief spell of silence after the children have gone to school. It's not like prose fiction where the writer has to plan or non-fiction where, for God's sake, the author has to do *research*. Poetry just comes, falling down out of the ether. And if you get yourself into the right poetic frame of mind you can catch it and make it come out of the end of your pen. To prove the point the poet Ian Macmillan once sat in a radio studio and told his listening audience that he was going to spend the next thirty seconds sending them by mind transfer the text of the poem he held in front of him. Listeners were asked to record what they received and to report back. Macmillan made his head as empty as he could and for the next half a minute stared at a blank sheet of paper. When he'd finished the phone began to ring and the fax to whirl. People turned up at the studio bearing copies of what they'd 'received'. Poetry for nothing, out of nowhere. All you do is write. Verse has turned into a national obsession. People use it to illustrate memories, to record events and to sort out those difficult blobs of emotion they have rolling around inside. Get your problems down as poetry and that will sort them out.

As an innocent pastime the activity has grown out of all proportions. In the past people were content to record their thoughts in private journals. Now they want them published. Untried, untutored, bashed out with only the slightest of concern for craft and off they go for publication. Am I being negative here? I am. Verse is no free handout and it is certainly not the easy route. Poets should work at their pieces for a lot longer before they declare them done. It's as if most of them have bought a violin on the way home, scratched a few cursory notes and then sent in their applications to join the LSO. In

123

any event, as a breed poets overproduce. There is too much verse on the market with the result that its principal consumers usually end up being the poets themselves. For an average new poetry pamphlet with a circulation of 200 copies the vast majority will either go unread into the system of archive, review and copyright copies or be bought as a matter of obligation by the poet's friends, colleagues and family.

If poets as part of their practice read more widely and felt some kind of obligation to support the system they have become part of then things could improve. Nothing runs in a vacuum, not least verse.

The scene

In response to this vast and constant production the UK poetry publishing scene is hardly a lean profit-hungry machine. At the top there are the commercial publishers. As ever, few in number and with tight, well-edited lists that seem to offer few opportunities for beginners. Faber & Faber take on the occasional new voice but it is never you. OUP run a broad list but always by authors you don't know. Dent want to make money; they publish R.S.Thomas. Below the mainstream operators lie the specialists. There are around half a dozen small, independent companies in the UK which were set up – often with grant aid – specifically to bring out new verse. Bloodaxe, Carcanet, Anvil, Seren, Stride and Peterloo are some of them. Here poetry gets a good bite of the cherry with solid, well-designed productions, usually commercially distributed and generally available throughout the Waterstone's and Dillons of the land. On the fringes Scotland, Wales and Ireland run their own, similar operations. All covered, you may think. What more could a poet want? Unfortunately these few business-like operators are nowhere near enough to satisfy demand.

The bulk of UK poetry ends up getting published not by professionals but by the hundreds of small and often one-person presses situated everywhere from Lewes to Llandudno, most of them unconcerned if their operations turn a profit or not. Small presses are of all types and sizes and often with wonderful names. Spectacular Diseases, Winter Sweet, Hangman Books, Kropotkin's Lighthouse Publications. Here poetry appears in both monolithic all-encompassing tomes and fleeting two-page pamphlets. Distribution can be worldwide or confined to the editor's friends at the pub. One small press I know tries deliberately *not* to sell, imagining that in the future, by virtue of their rarity, the value of its books will increase.

You can find many small presses detailed in the writers' guides. There is a good list in *The Writer's Handbook*. Specialist directories include Oriel's *Small Presses and Little Magazines of the UK and Ireland* (TSO Oriel, The Friary, Cardiff CF1 4AA) and the catalogue put out by the ALP, the Association of Little Presses (see Appendix One for more information).

What makes a poetry book?

Unlike novels or works of local history a book of poems has no obligation to look like a book at all. In fact a good many do not. Poetry is the one area where experimentation with the form of the book abounds. Because sales and commerce are not the main aim, and in many cases not an aim at all, anything is possible. Poets have provided the UK public with some of the weirdest, most innovative and most exciting examples of book art available anywhere. I have seen poetry collections bound between pieces of carpet, sheets of metal, and once between bits of wood with sandals affixed and held together with metal bolts. Books come in boxes, in packets, in envelopes with added objects, or with coloured film overlays and inserted transparencies. I was presented with one Fluxus item contained in a family-size matchbox. Within were the sections of the work each contained in a smaller box. At the memorably named Strange Faeces Press the poet Opal L. Nations solved the problem of thin editions vanishing on people's shelves. He bound wire coat hangers in the spines of his so they could be stored in the wardrobe along with the shirts. Glenn Carmichael's Pimp$ of the Alphabet Press produces editions which are held together not with thread but with brightly coloured and very visible pink ribbon. A matter of style, he says.

Poetry titles are hardly ever restricted by needing to be of standard extent. Five hundred poems or five are just the same. Both can be set up to make a book. It is an area where the pamphlet reigns supreme. So long as you can justify yourself by fine production or the need of your one or two chosen poems for space to breathe then all is OK. You'd like a book out but you've only one forty-line item plus a couple of haikus? It won't make much but go ahead.

There are norms, naturally. Many poetry collections, known as slim volumes, run to between thirty- or forty-page-long poems plus a short biographical note on the author. Check out the poetry section at your local bookshop, looking at the output of new titles from OUP, Bloodaxe or Cape.

125

Co-operation

The boundary between self-publisher and small press blurs in the poetry world. As we've seen, many poets looking for ways to get their own work out end up publishing pamphlets by others and almost by default find themselves founding a publishing operation. It is the logical way to do things. Poetry seems to operate better in a milieu than in isolation. The financial arrangements between author and small publisher are also at considerable variance with those of their more commercial partners. Small presses are never in action for profit; they publish for reasons of obsession or culture. Money is scarce. Books and booklets are often accepted on the understanding that production will go ahead only if a grant can be had from the local Arts Board or if the poet is also able to help.

This help can be in the form of personal financial subsidy, assistance with production and distribution or, as if often the case, both. Small presses work much more closely with their authors than do their commercial counterparts. Rupert Loydell at Stride reckons that production can only ever go ahead if the poet is able to guarantee sales in some way. The author needs to be out there giving readings, knocking on the doors of bookshops and flogging copies hand to hand. How much the final edition remains entirely a product of the small press or a self-published item in its own right is a matter for debate. Not every small press works this way. Some are happy to publish the whole thing themselves and reward their authors with free copies along with whatever reviews they can pull. Others with agreed grant aid run regular publishing programmes that involve their authors in more traditional promotion rather than having them act as surrogate reps. But if it's poetry you publish expect to get involved.

Beware

Naturally poetry publishing is also the field most tilled by the vanity operators (see Chapter Three). Because conditions vary so much it is often very hard for the beginner to tell if the operator with whom they are contracting is a genuine small press asking for, perhaps, £100 or so to ensure a decent cover or a shark biting off a several thousand pounds in exchange for half a day's work. Ask to see previous examples of the press's output, check with the Association of Little Presses (see Appendix One) and if it still sounds bad ring the best vanity vigilante we currently have, Johnathon Clifford, on 01329 822218.

Actual self-publishing

After all this you may wonder what the advantages of using someone else's small press for your book actually are. Why not do the whole thing on your own? Yet working with others, even at this level, does have its advantages. No matter how small they are, small presses will have published other titles before and will know something of how the scene works. Publishing in the company of others can add credibility to your title. But if you do want to strike out alone then a pamphlet of self-published poetry is probably the easiest place to start. Check things to see what others do. The tradition is a strong one. Ask at your local bookshop or contact the ALP who publish a catalogue of members' titles. There are also a number of specialist poetry booksellers who can provide examples by mail. These include:

Alan Halsey / The Poetry Bookshop, West House, Broad Street, Hay-on-Wye HR3 5DB (Tel: 01497 820 305).

Paul Green, 83(b) London Road, Peterborough, Cambs PE2 9BS.

Peter Riley Books, 27 Sturton Street, Cambridge CB1 2QC (Tel: 01223 327455).

For more information on the poetry scene and poetry publishing consult my own *The Poetry Business* (Seren Books), Paul Hyland's *Getting Into Poetry* (Bloodaxe) or Peter Sansom's excellent *Writing Poems* (Bloodaxe).

18

IF IT CAN GO WRONG, IT WILL

Writing, publishing and then selling what you've done can be a complex business and there are plenty of opportunities for things to go wrong. If you proceed carefully, most blunders can be guarded against but there is always the unexpected. What do you do when things don't turn out quite as planned?

Printer's errors

When the books first arrive from the printer and you've got one out of the packet, the chances are that it won't look quite how you imagined it. This is normal: there are always subtle variations between concept and final product. The problems begin if the books don't look like what you wanted at all.

Variations are of two types: first what you've got is not what you ordered and second what you've got is what you ordered but badly done. The easier of the two to resolve is the former. If you ordered a gloss art board and what you've been given is matt; or the paper was to be 115-gsm smooth cartridge and the books have been printed on 80-gsm plain; or you wanted a squared, perfect-bound spine and you've been sent a wire-stitched job, then it's wrong. Check the facts. Refer to the printer's estimate and to your written order for the job. Be absolutely certain that you have agreed to no changes during the course of production and left nothing to the choice of others. Prove that there is an error and prove that it is not yours. Then contact the printer and ask him what he intends to do.

It may be an obvious mistake on their part which they will admit to immediately. On the other hand it may be necessary to convince them. If everything is in writing, as it ought to be, then you should have no difficulty. Beware talk of the job being 'more or less' what was ordered – printing specifications are always precise. Guard against the old excuse – the change of plan which you are reputed to have agreed to over the phone at the last minute. If you ordered yellow paper then that is what you wanted. Dig your heels in.

In these circumstances printers have two options – they can take the books back and reprint or they can make you an offer to accept them as they are and pay less for the job. You decide.

Things are less clearly defined if the problem is of the second type – the books appear badly done. This moves us into the area of acceptable standards of production and it is more true than ever these days that you get what you pay for. A defence is to claim the job as 'commercially acceptable'. If you don't happen to find it so then you may be in for a hard time. Certain things will be inarguably obvious – the binding may fall apart, the imposition may be out of true. Others are vaguer – the colour of the cover is not quite right, the pages look cramped, in some places the print appears smudged. Point out these failings. You will have checked the printer's capabilities by viewing samples of his work before accepting the original quotation. Draw attention to this. Be polite but firm.

Imperfections which do not affect the whole print run are far more common and far harder to spot. Individual books can be faulty. They may be misbound, have blank pages, missing sections or incorrectly aligned illustrations, or be badly trimmed. Such errors are generally not identified at the time of delivery but only come to light later as the stock is being sold. Trade practice on printer's or binder's imperfections of this kind is for the publisher to be reimbursed at 30 per cent of the original published price or for the imperfection to be made good – whatever the manufacturer decides. With a small number of copies out of a run of a few hundred, you'll probably be paid; if half the batch have the middle section bound in upside-down then the printer will have them redone.

It is also common for the quantity delivered to be slightly at variance with the quantity ordered. This is usual and will be covered in the small print on the back of your estimate. If you are a large number of copies short, report this to the printer immediately.

The relationship you establish with your printer is important. It should be friendly but businesslike. Remember that there are no favours in business no matter how things sounded when they were being arranged. Check everything and only when you are completely happy turn your attention to the bill. In the case of a dispute, the only customer with any clout is the one who hasn't yet paid.

Publisher's errors

More expensive and much harder to manage are mistakes which are clearly your own. If it is one of design then you have to live with it. Certain things such as the binding and perhaps the cover board could be changed but you would have to pay. If the error is typographical, there is a mistake in the text or a section left out, then an *erratum slip*

– a printed correction – can be prepared and either inserted somewhere among the prelims or actually stuck across the offending page. In some cases, erratum slips draw attention to errors which may otherwise pass unnoticed. Be sure the blunder is big enough to make a fuss about.

Misprints are best avoided in the first place, of course, but don't be unduly worried if you are forced into having to put a sticker somewhere. It happens to the best of commercial publishers. It has been known for complete chapters to be omitted and in one or two cases for even the name on the cover to be wrong.

Other difficulties with which to contend

- The printer is late delivering the book. There is very little you can do. A recent survey among small and medium-sized publishers showed that virtually no one consistently got their book stock delivered on time. It is in the nature of things that at some point in the production process a key person will have to choose between your job and that of a large and important customer in a hurry. If you want guarantees on delivery dates then the only way of being really sure is for you to print the books yourself.
- You've overpriced the book. Your chosen price which covers costs turns out to make the book far too expensive to sell. You should have spotted this at the planning stage but didn't. Either acknowledge it now and reduce the price which will at least shift the books, or try to cut your expenses. Could you sell the book yourself rather than use a distributor? Could you sell direct to the reader rather than use bookshops? Whatever you do, the answer is not to stick it out. The overly expensive book will simply not be bought.
- Bookshops refuse to stock it. Whatever the book, not every shop will want it on their shelves but if you are consistently refused you should attempt to find out why. Any one of a number of things from the price to the subject matter could be at fault. If you discover that your book on how to make love underwater is being rejected on moral grounds then you have no option but to abandon the retail trade. If, however, it is more a matter of the cover design then you can always print a plain dust-wrapper and go in for a cover-up. Local sensibilities should always be considered if you want to make sales.
- Another publisher comes out with what is clearly a better book on the same subject. Happens all the time. Despite the good intentions of the various registers which enable writers to cross-check that they are not researching a subject already the province of

someone else, large numbers of books on Scott of the Antarctic continue to be published simultaneously. Rather than be worried by this, welcome it. Ride on the back of the interest in the subject generated by the other's publicity. In the trade this is called 'me too'. Tell everyone that your book is really the better one. Competition always increases total sales. As long as the subject is not too specialist, you'll weather the storm.

- Your launch publicity is obscured by a national disaster which swamps the media. An act of God against which there is no protection. You have little option but to scrap the publication date, rethink the campaign and launch the book again. Beware, though, of planning your launch for the same time as a known event. Check *Whitaker's Almanack*. General elections are best avoided.

- Sales are slow and your faith in the project thins. Perhaps you have misjudged the market. But if there have been some sales then there can be more. By their nature, certain titles take time to build up steam. Put greater effort into promotion, send out extra review copies and keep going.

- Costs spiral as you proceed. You've miscalculated the price of promotion, forgotten about despatch charges or misread the printer's original quotation. Re-price – a common occurrence in the book trade and much more frequent in times of inflation. To make it official, have a sticker produced which incorporates both your name as publisher and the new price. Remember to fix these to the books before distribution.

- Your story of the town records a humorous if slightly dubious incident in the Mayor's past and you are accused of libel. This can be very worrying. Go straight to your solicitor. If your anecdote turns out to be true then the libel action will become an enormous boost. Sales will treble. But always be sure of your facts.

- You get bad reviews. Should you respond? Much depends on the nature of the criticism being made. Errors of fact can be corrected by writing a letter, for publication, to the editor of the paper or magazine concerned. If the criticism is more personal then a response on your part may serve only to prolong the situation. However you phrase your justification, the reviewer will always have the last word. No matter how incensed you feel at the time it is best to bite your tongue and do nothing. Bad reviews pass. Try not to give the critics the opportunity to state their case a second time.

- You are a huge success. Far greater and far swifter than you ever expected. The books sell out within a week. Should you reprint?

Check first that it actually has sold out and isn't simply sitting quietly in a stockroom somewhere just waiting for time to pass so it can be packed up and returned. Have you been paid by everyone for the sales of the first edition? If you have then you are a real success and assuming you have costed your book accordingly, will now have a small profit to prove it.

Reprints should not be entered into lightly. Your first edition may have completely satisfied initial demand. But if you are convinced there is a further market then it will certainly be a profitable one. Reprints are a fraction of the cost of the initial project. Once the decision has been made, move swiftly. Keep the books on the boil.

If sales are steady rather than dramatic and you envisage a reprint but not for some time then it is worth asking the printer to keep the plates used for your job. Litho plates remain the property of the printer and are, in practice, normally destroyed. If you wish them to be kept indefinitely there may be a storage charge. You, as publisher, are the owner of any letterpress plates, blocks, film or computer disks used in production. If you'd like these items returned, you must let the printer know.

● It doesn't sell. What are your options? You have three: you can push the copies under the bed or in the bin and forget about them (Richard Booth, owner of one of the world's largest second-hand bookshops in the town of books, Hay-on-Wye, disposes of his unselling surpluses by distributing them to the poor and aged of the district as fuel for their fires); you can give them away – triple your review list, present a copy to every friend and acquaintance, put a copy in with every letter you write; or, finally, you can reduce the price. Small slivers knocked off will make little difference – the cut has to be substantial. Half-price or less and even then the going will still be hard.

The ultimate act is to remainder them. A dealer in surplus books will buy every copy you have. Ask for 10p a copy and be satisfied with less. In the old days, copies would be quietly shipped and discreetly disposed of abroad. Today your failure will be broadcast to all with your title appearing on remainder tables across the country at an embarrassingly knock-down price. Dealers in remainders advertise regularly in *The Bookseller*. There is also a list of them in Cassell's *Directory of Publishing*. They buy almost anything. Send a sample and a note saying how many copies you have.

● The whole project has been a failure. This can be depressing but you will have learned something even if it is only how to do it correctly a second time. The biggest disasters are usually the result of a flawed concept. Few will admit to them. Stella Meredith, who self-published a Second World War spy novel, *The Last Snows of Winter*, sold only a few dozen copies and lost nearly £2,000. This seems a lot; even the most badly marketed novel ought to do better. It transpired that the author's purpose in publishing had not been primarily to sell the story as a book at all but rather to promote it to television as the basis for a film. The plan didn't work. Despite a good print job and an attractive cover, the novel floundered. There was no marketing, no promotion and no reviews – failure was total. Chastened but undaunted, Stella Meredith is now recasting the tale as a stage play. The novels are in a box out the back.

Such debacles are rare and by planning most can be avoided. But you must know a little of books and their readers before you begin.

Anyone who writes a book and doesn't expect aggravation should forget about writing the book.

Bill Adler

For some writers, self-publishing will be the only way of achieving their goal, for others merely the best way. Whatever your reasons now is the time to begin.

APPENDIX ONE
ORGANISATIONS OF INTEREST TO SELF-PUBLISHERS

The Association of Little Presses was formed in 1966 as a 'loosely knit association of individuals running little presses who have grouped together for mutual self-help'. It acted at first as a pressure group to extend the availability of grant aid and later as an information exchange, advice centre and general promoter of the movement. Strongly, though not exclusively, biased towards creative writing, ALP currently represents some 250 publishers and associations throughout Britain and Ireland. Membership costs £12.50 and is open to both presses and interested individuals. Self-publishers are actively encouraged to join. The Association produces a catalogue of *Small Press Books in Print*; a magazine *PALPI (Poetry and Little Press Information)*, which gives details of recent activity; an *ALP Newsletter* of printing and distribution tips; plus various information sheets. On a regular basis, ALP organises book fairs, exhibitions and gatherings around the country, and offers an unrivalled service, by post and telephone, giving information on how you can publish yourself and what you can do with it when you have. The ALP web site is at http://www.melloworld.com/alp/. The ALP co-ordinator is Chris Jones at 111 Banbury Road, Oxford OX2 6JX (01865 511186). Vice President is Bob Cobbing at 89(a) Petherton Road, London N5 2QT (0171 226 2657).

The Author-Publisher Network is an association of writers who publish, or intend to publish, and market their own work. It is open to any writer, artist or poet who wishes to take control of the whole process of publishing their own books. The A-PN, known originally as the Author-Publisher Enterprise, was the brainchild of technical author John Dawes. It was formed in 1992. Members of A-PN share information and ideas and attend association seminars, workshops and book fairs. The organisation publishes a most useful magazine, *Write to Publish*, under the editorship of Daphne Macara, along with a series of pamphlets including *Selling Books by Direct Mail, Useful Contacts for Self-publishers, a Directory of Members*, and a regular *Catalogue of Member's Books*. The A-PN acts as a clearing house for orders for members' titles. A-PN also produces various *Guidelines* on subjects of specific interest. Daphne Macara's *Small Publishers A–Z; the Guide to Good Publishing* (A-PN/Pandor House Publications) is particularly good. The organisation is hot on electronic pre-press and the opportunities presented by the Internet. Membership costs £15.00. A-PN secretary is Daphne Macara, 6 Kelvinbrook, Hurst Park, West Molesey, Surrey KT8 1RZ (0181 979 3060).

The Independent Publishers Guild was founded in 1962 to offer a forum for the exchange of ideas and information among small and non-aligned publishers. A number of its members have begun as self-publishers. It produces a regular *Bulletin*; mounts an annual weekend conference; and runs seminars on a variety of topics. These have recently included business planning and finance; publishing law; printing, type-setting and the new technology; book design; and promoting and publicity. At present full membership is only open to publishers who have produced more than three titles. Newcomers can join as non-voters. The IPG is a lively, forward-looking organisation which provides an ideal point of contact for self-publishers with a commercial bent. Membership costs £88.13. IPG secretary is Yvonne Messenger, 25 Cambridge Road, Hampton, Middlesex TW12 2JL (0181 979 0250).

The Book Trust was founded in 1925. It is an independent educational charity promoting books and reading and includes Young Book Trust (formerly the Children's Book Foundation). The Trust offers a book information service; administers many literary prizes (including the Booker Prize, and the Orange Prize for Fiction); carries out surveys; publishes useful reference books and resource materials; houses a children's book reference library; and promotes children's books through activities such as Children's Book Week. Membership costs £25. Executive Director is Brian Perman, Book House, 45 East Hill, London SW18 2QZ (0181 870 9055).

Book Publishing Books, a division of Book House Training Centre, the professional training organisation, offers a comprehensive mail-order service in the field of books relating to publishing. BPB can supply works on everything from the history of book manufacture to multilingual dictionaries of copyright, rights and contractual terms. Send for its free catalogue. BPB Administrator, 45 East Hill, London SW18 2QZ (0181 874 2718).

British Printing Industries Federation is the professional organisation for UK printers. Of interest to self-publishers are its lists of members and its *Publications for Printers* catalogue and supply service. Contact it at 11 Bedford Row, London WC1R 4DX (0171 242 6904).

The David Thomas Charitable Trust Self-publishing Awards are worth at least £1,000 annually. Awards are made in four categories:

fiction, non-fiction, poetry and children's books. David Thomas, one of the founders of the publishers, David & Charles, now runs the magazine, *Writers News*, amongst other things a regular source of information for self-publishers. Details of the charitable awards can be had from Lorna Edwards, Competitions and Awards Manager, Writers News, PO Box 4, Nairn IV12 4HU (01667 45441).

The Society of Authors, 84 Drayton Gardens, London SW10 9SB (0171 373 6642). Primarily a trade union for professional writers and concerns itself with the whole spectrum of authorship, supplying information and advice on the practice of writing and representing members' interests to employers, usually publishers, much in the way other trade unions do. The Society is a professional body providing service of the highest order. It publishes a magazine, *The Author*, which includes articles on all aspects of writing and on publishing. Membership fees begin at £52.

Password Training, New Mount Street, Manchester M4 4DE (0161 953 4009) provides specialist training courses for self-publishers in various aspects of production, finance, production planning, marketing, design, direct marketing and publishing on the Internet. Password offers a consultancy service and can direct applicants towards sources of grant aid. Send for its leaflets. The organisation's web site is at http://www.poptel.org.uk/password/training.html

Scottish Publishers Association, Scottish Book Centre, 137 Dundee Street, Edinburgh EH11 1BG (0131 228 6866). Open for membership to anyone publishing books in Scotland, the Association mounts joint exhibits at bookfairs and trade shows; publishes seasonal catalogues; a list of members; and issues regular newsletters. Members range from multinationals to one-person operations. If your base is Scotland it is worth enquiring. Director is Lorraine Fannin.

Welsh Books Council, Castell Brychan, Aberystwyth, Ceredigion SY23 2JB (01970 624151). This is a government-funded body established to promote the writing and marketing of books in Wales. It has departments dealing with design, editing, publicity and marketing and maintains the Welsh Books Centre, a comprehensive warehouse, representation and distribution service for books of Welsh interest or origin in both English and Welsh. Self-publishers with appropriate books will find the Book Centre's distribution services within Wales unrivalled. The Council publishes booklists and a quarterly journal, *Llais Llyrfau/ Book News*. Becoming a Friend of the Welsh Books Council will cost you £10 annually.

APPENDIX TWO
BOOKS OF INTEREST TO SELF-PUBLISHERS

History and background

Bill Adler: *Inside Publishing*, Bobbs-Merrill 1982

B. E. Bellamy: *Private Presses and Publishing in England Since 1945*, Clive Bingley 1982

Anthony Blond: *The Book Book*, Jonathan Cape 1985

Victor Bonham-Carter: *Authors by Profession*, Society of Authors 1978

Johnathon Clifford: *Vanity Press and the Proper Poetry Publishers*, The Author 1994

Gerald Donaldson: *Books*, Phaidon 1981

John Feather: *A History of British Book Publishing*, Routledge 1991

Geoffrey Ashall Glaister: *Encyclopaedia of the Book*, British Library 1979

Richard Kennedy: *A Boy at the Hogarth Press*, Penguin 1978

Eric Lane: *Dante Alighieri's Publishing Company*, Dedalus 1985

Michael Legat: *An Author's Guide To Publishing*, Hale 1982

Peter H. Mann: *From Author to Reader: a Social Study of Books*, Routledge 1982

Ian Norrie: *Mumby's Publishing and Bookselling in the Twentieth Century*, Bell & Hyman 1982

Peter Owen (ed): *Publishing Now*, Peter Owen 1993

S. H. Steinberg: *Five Hundred Years of Printing*, Penguin 1955

Sir Stanley Unwin: *The Truth about Publishing*, George Allen & Unwin 1926

Ken Warpole: *Reading by Numbers: Contemporary Publishing and Popular Fiction*, Comedia 1984

Ken Warpole and Dave Morley (eds): *The Republic of Letters: Working-class Writing and Local Publishing*, Comedia 1982

Copy preparation, layout and book design

Jill Baker: *Copy Prep*, Blueprint 1987

Geoff Barlow and Simon Eccles: *Typesetting and Composition*, Blueprint 1992

Fernard Baudin: *How Typography Works*, Lund Humphreys 1989

Judith Butcher: *Copy-Editing*, Cambridge University Press 1992

Gillian Clarke: *Basic Proof-reading*, BHTC 1992

Martin Colyer: *Commissioning Illustration*, Phaidon 1990
Charles Foster: *Editing, Design and Book Production*, Pluto Press 1993
Nicola Harris: *Basic Editing*, BHTC 1991
Hart's Rules – for Compositors and Readers, OUP 1983
Ruari Mclean: *The Thames and Hudson Manual of Typography*, Thames and Hudson 1992
The Oxford Dictionary for writers and Editors, OUP 1981
James Sutton and Alan Bartram: *Typefaces for Books*, British Library, 1990
Robin Williams: *The Non-Designer's Design Book*, Peachpit Press 1994
Hugh Williamson: *Methods of Book Design*, Yale 1983

Indexing and copyright

J. M. Cavendish and Kate Pool: *Handbook of Copyright in British Publishing Practice*, Cassell 1993
Ruth Cannedy Cross: *Indexing Books*, World Guild Books 1980
Michael Henry: *Publishing and Media Law*, Butterworth 1994
G. N. Knight: *The Art of Indexing*, Allen and Unwin 1979
Raymond A. Wall: *Copyright Made Easier*, ASLIB 1993

Printing and home publishing

Charles N. Aronson: *The Writer Publisher*, Charles N. Aronson 1976
David Bann: *The Print Production Handbook*, Little, Brown and Company 1994
Michael Barnard: *Introduction to Printing Processes*, Blueprint 1991
M. Barnard, J. Peacock and C. Berrill: *The Pindar Pocket Print Production Guide*, Blueprint 1995
Clifford Burke: *Printing It*, Wingbow 1972
Michael Scott Cain: *The Co-Op Publishing Handbook*, Dustbooks 1978
Peter Domanski and Philip Irvine: *A Practical Guide to Publishing Books Using Your PC*, Domanski-Irvine Books 1997.
Bill Henderson (ed): *The Publish-It-Yourself Handbook: Literary Tradition and How-To*, Pushcart Book Press 1973
Graham Jones: *How to Publish a Newsletter*, How To Books 1992
Ann Kritzinger: *Brief Guide to Self-Publishing*, Scriptmate Editions 1991
Roy Lewis and John B. Easson: *Publishing and Printing at Home*, David & Charles 1984

Daphne Macara: *Small Publishers A-Z*, Pandor House 1996
L. W. Mueller: *How to Publish Your Own Book*, Harlo Press 1976
Harry Mulholland: *Guide to Self-Publishing*, Mulholland Wirral 1984
John Peacock: *Book Production*, Blueprint 1995
Dan Poynter: *The Self-Publishing Manual*, Para Publishing 1995
Pamela Richmond: *Bookbinding: a Manual of Techniques*, Crowood
    Press, 1995
Robert Spicer: *How to Publish a Book*, How To Books 1993
Tom and Marilyn Ross: *The Complete Guide to Self-Publishing*,
    Writer's Digest Books 1994
Ian Templeton: *Publish it Yourself and Make it Pay*, Pikers Pad 1985
Audrey and Philip Ward: *The Small Publisher*, Oleander 1979
Celeste West and Valerie Wheat: *The Passionate Perils of Publishing*,
    Booklegger 1978
Jonathan Zeitlyn: *Print: How You Can Do It Yourself*, Journeyman
    Press 1992

Sales, marketing and promotion

Michael Barnard and Ray Webb: *The Book Distribution Handbook*,
    Pira International 1995
Alison Baverstock: *How To Market Books*, Kogan Page 1996
Alison Baverstock: *Common-sense Marketing for Non-Marketers*,
    Piatkus 1995
Bill Godber, Robert Wenn and Keith Smith: *Marketing for Small
    Publishers*, Journeyman Press 1992
Ros Jay: *Teach Yourself Marketing Your Small Business*, Hodder &
    Stoughton 1996
Denis MacShane: *Using the Media*, Pluto 1983
David Northmore: *How to Get Publicity for Free*, Bloomsbury 1993
Terry Prone: *Just a Few Words*, Poolbeg 1989

Desk-top publishing, multimedia and electronic publishing

Brian and Margot Blunden: *The Electronic Publishing Business and
    Its Market*, Pira International 1994
Fabrizio Cafferelli: *Publish Yourself on CD-Rom: Mastering CDs for
    Multimedia*, Random House Electronic 1993
Brian Cookman: *Desktop Design – Getting the Professional Look*,
    Blueprint 1993
Jane Dorner: *Writing on Disk*, John Taylor Book Ventures 1992
Jill H. Ellsworth and Matthew V. Ellsworth: *Marketing on the Internet*,
    1995

Neil Fawcett: *Teach Yourself Multimedia*, Hodder & Stoughton 1994

Tony Feldman: *Multimedia*, Blueprint 1993

David Hewson: *Introduction to Desktop Publishing*, John Taylor Book Ventures 1988

Vera Hughes: *Teach Yourself Word Processing*, Hodder & Stoughton 1992

Paul Ulna: *Understanding Type for Desktop Publishing*, Blueprint 1992

Mac Bride: *Teach Yourself the Internet*, Hodder & Stoughton 1995

Mac Bride: *Teach Yourself HTML – Publishing on the World Wide Web*, Hodder & Stoughton 1996

Sue Schofield: *The UK Internet Book*, Addison-Wesley 1995

Directories

See comprehensive list in Chapter Fifteen.

INDEX

Abse, Dannie 19
acknowledgements 6, 40-1, 42-3, 66
Adams, Richard 19
Adler, Bill 3, 105, 133, 137
Allen, George 8
AmiPro 46, 89
Amra Editions 65
anatomy 39-44
Antony Rowe Limited 84
Anvil Press 124
appendices 43
Arrow 14
art board 72, 78, 128
Arts Councils 29, 117
ASCII 46
Association for Business Sponsorship of
the Arts 30
Association of Little Presses iii, 76, 126,
134
Austen, Jane 6
author's corrections 58
Author-Publisher Enterprise 24, 121,
134-5

bad reviews 131
Balzac, Honoré de 7
banks 28
bar codes 36
Barton, David 20-1
bastard-title 40
Bellamy, B. E. 137
beyond the book 116-18
binding 16, 64, 75-6, 82
Bingley, Clive 137
Binns, Richard 96, 112-13
black lettering 72
Blackburn, Michael 119
Blackwell's 14
Blake, William 4, 10, 66
bleeding 81
Blond, Anthony 4-5, 61, 137
Bloodaxe 124, 125, 127
Blueprint 75
blurb 47-8, 72, 107
Bonura, Larry S. 43
Book Publishing Books 135
Book Trust 135
Bookbank 36
Booker Prize 22, 23, 54, 135
book-keeping 34-5
Books Etc. 14

Booth, Richard 132
Boswell, James 13
Bradt, George 76
British Library 16, 37, 103, 104
British Library Cataloguing-in-
Publication Data Programme 37,
40
British National Bibliography 103
British Printing Industries Federation 81,
135
British Printing Society 68, 76
British Standard BS 5261 58
bromide 70
Bryson, Bill 33
Burdelt, Eric 76
Burns, Robert 7
business names 31-2
Butcher, Judith 81, 137
Byron, Lord 7

Cambridge University Press 81
Cape, Jonathan 27, 125
Carcanet 124
Carmichael, Glenn 125
Cassell 100, 132
Caxton 4
CD-ROM 40, 90, 92, 119
Centaur Press 113
Chapman, Robin 27, 96
chapter headings 62, 63
Chernaik, Judith 117
Clement, Aeron 19-20
Clifford, Johnathon 16, 126, 137
club lines 62
Cobbing, Bob 22, 74
collectives 76
colour 64, 65-6, 72, 78, 117
colour photocopier 66
Colt Books 23
Companies House 31-2
computers 45, 50, 61, 71, 72, 79, 86-7,
88-92, 118-22
contents 42
Cookman, Brian 91, 139
Coombs, D. 80
copyright 6-7, 12, 32-3, 40, 103
copyright libraries 103-4
Corgi 14
covers 14, 21, 47-8, 59, 64-6, 67, 71-2,
78, 107, 117, 125, 130
crop marks 80, 89

cummings, e.e. 114
Curtis, Tony 123

Dahn, Felix 93
Daily Mirror 16
David & Charles 76, 136
David Thomas Charitable Trust Self-
    publishing Awards 135-6
Davies, W. H. 7
Dawes, John 24, 134
dedication 41-2
delivery note 95-6
Dent, J. M. 124
design 59-66, 83-4, 90
Designs and Patents Act 1988 32
Desktop publishing 22, 88-92
despatch 102
Dickens, Charles 6, 117
Dillons 14, 98, 99, 124
direct selling 102-3, 107
discounts to booksellers 8, 94, 98, 99-
    100
distribution costs 94, 95
distributors and freelance reps 96, 100-1
DocuTech 55, 86, 87
doing some of it yourself 68
Donleavy, J. P. 2
Dorner, Jane 88, 121, 139
Druid Press 19
duplicator 73-4

Egerton, Thomas 6
electronic publishing 118-20
Eliot, T. S. 12
Ellis, Ron 31, 32, 95, 97
Encarta 119-20
Encyclopaedia Britannica 93
end matter 39, 43-4, 64
Ex-Libris Press 25, 85

Faber & Faber 20, 25, 124
famous poets 71
Fanthorpe, Lionel 21
fax-on-demand 118
Felton, Mick iv
film 71
finishing 5, 53, 67, 68, 72-3
Finlay, Ian Hamilton 22
firm sale 99-100
Fitzgerald, Edward 7
Fluxus 125
flyers 107-8
folding 69, 72-3
foreword 42
Foster, Charles 61, 81, 138
four-colour process 3, 5, 78
Freeman, Bobby 47

Gaberbocchus 20

Galsworthy, John 7
Gerhardi, Helga 21
Germ, The 114
Green Bay Publications 23
Greene, Alan 116
Gregynog Press 75
Grey, Zane 7
Griffiths, Bill 65
guillotines 73, 89
Gutenberg 6

half-title 40, 64
Hammicks 14
Hangman Books 124
hardback bindings 82
Hart's Rules 49, 138
Henderson, Bill 1, 138
Hidden, Norman 105
home binding 5, 75-6
home letterpress 74-5
home litho 5, 69, 75
home pages 120
Hopkinson, Anthony 68
Houghton Mifflin 23
house style 49
How To Books 27, 116
how to find a printer 55-6
how to publish your poetry 123-7
HTML 121, 122
hype 112-13
hyper text 121

illustrations 42, 51, 52, 64, 65, 71, 72,
    78-81, 89
imagesetters 70-1, 89
imposition 69-70, 71
independent publishers 4, 17
Independent Publishers Guild 135
index 43-4
International Standard Book Numbers
    35-6, 40, 116
International Standard Serial Numbers
    116
Internet 120-2, 135
invoice 95-6
ISBN iii, 35-6, 40, 116
ISBN Agency 35

James, Huw iv
James, Keith iv, 84
Java 122
jogger 73
John Taylor Book Ventures 139
Johnson, Arthur W. 76
Jones, Graham 116, 138
Jones, Roger 25
Journeyman Press 61, 81
Joyce, James 2, 8
justified type 61, 70

INDEX

Kelmscott Press 10-11, 62
kerning 61, 83
Kindredson Publishing 20
Kipling, Rudyard 7
Knowles, Ron iv
Kogan Page 116
Kritzinger, Ann 24, 138
Kropotkin's Lighthouse Publications 124

Lamb, Charles 109
Lane, Eric 97, 104, 137
lap-top computers 91-2
Larkin, Philip 7
laser printer 70
launches 110, 131
Lawrence, D. H. 9-10
Legat, Michael 5, 137
letterpress 55, 77
libel 34, 131
light pens 92
Linotype 45
list of illustrations 42
listings 110-12
Local Enterprise Agencies 30
Local Enterprise Councils 30
Lottery and pools money 29
Luben, Jacquelyn 24

McLean, Ruari 61, 138
magazine publishing 114-16
Marcan, Peter 96-7
marketing 4, 14, 21, 25, 46-9, 54, 105-13
Menzies 14, 97, 98, 99
Meredith, Stella 133
Microsoft 92, 119, 120
Mills, Christopher 66
mistakes 45, 49-50, 57-8
Mo, Timothy 22
mock-up 52, 57, 83
Morning Star Publications 22
Morris, William 10-11, 62
Mulholland, Harry 43, 69, 96, 139
multimedia 119
Murray, John 6

Nations, Opal L. 125
New Yorker, The 11
Nin, Anaïs 11-12
Northmore, David 108

offset-litho 55, 77, 88, 132
Oleander Press 17, 25
Oriel 125
origination 27, 53, 67, 69, 88
Ottakars 14
overpricing 130
Oxford University Press 4, 49, 106, 119, 124, 125
Ozzard, Chris 66

page sizes 67
PageMaker 91
Paine, Thomas 7
Palmer, Terry 24-5
Pan 14
Pandora Press 66
Pandya, Michael 3
Papanek, Victor 59
paper 4, 27, 57, 63-4, 67, 68, 77
Para Publishing 118
Password Training 136
paste-up 5, 69, 80, 88
Penguin 1, 14, 19, 48, 67, 102
perfect binding 64, 75-6, 128
Peterloo Poets 124
phone selling 99, 115
photocopy 66, 74, 86
Picador 48
Pimp$ of the Alphabet Press 125
Pira International 101
placing the order 57, 82
plagiarism 33-4
Poetry on the Underground 117
Pope, Alexander 7, 13
Potter, Beatrix 7
Pound, Ezra 12, 109
Poynter, Dan 118, 139
preface 42
preliminary matter 39, 40-3, 64
presentation copies 109-10
press releases 108-9
pricing 56, 67-76, 94-5
printer's errors 57-8, 128-9
Pritt Stick 69
private loans 31
private presses 17
proofs 43, 57-8, 71
Public Lending Right 39
publication dates 106-7, 109
Publisher's Association 100-1
publisher's errors 129-30
Pythia Books 113

QuarkXPress 91
quotations 56-7, 68, 84, 128

Radford, Roger 20
Ransom, Will 17
Red Sharks Press 66
Regional Arts Boards 28-9, 116
review copies 8, 16, 109, 132
Robinson, Edward Arlington 7
Rosenheim, Andrew 119
Ruskin, John 8

sale or return 98, 100
Sandburg, Carl 7
Scottish Publishers Association 136
scriveners 71

Second Aeon iii, 114
selling to bookshops iv, 96-9
Seren Books 125, 127
Sergeant, Howard 2
Shaw, George Bernard 13
Shelley, Percy Bysshe 9
short run production 67, 86-7
Simon, Herbert 59
Sinclair, Upton 7
Skeffington, Francis 8
small presses 14-15, 110, 125, 134
Smith, Keith 14
Smith, W. H. 4, 14, 18, 20, 97-8, 99
Society of Authors 121, 136
SoftKey 119
specialist self-publisher production house
84-6
Spectacular Diseases 124
Spiegl, Fritz 47
sponsorship 6, 28, 29-30, 115-16
spot-colour 66
Spray Mount 69
stapling 64, 72-3, 75, 77
statement 95-6
Stationer's Hall 34
Stein, Gertrude 7, 77, 81
Sterne, Laurence 12, 42
Story, Jack Trevor 7
Stride 124, 126
subscription 7, 115
subsidy publishers 15-16
subtitle 47
Sunk Island Review 119

talking books 117-18
tax 34-5
telephone answering machines 116
Thackeray, William Makepeace 7
Thames and Hudson 61
Themerson, Stephan 20
Thomas, R. S. 19, 124
Tipp-Ex 69
title 35-6, 47
title page 6, 40
Trading and Enterprise Councils 30
training 91
Transworld 23
Turley, Dr Raymond 23
Turner, Barry 29, 33
Twain, Mark 7
typefaces 41, 45, 46, 51, 59, 60-1, 72,
84, 88, 90

UNESCO 39
unjustified type 62
Unwin, Sir Stanley 33, 93, 137

vanity presses 15-16, 28, 85, 105, 126
VAT 34-5
Ventura 91
Village Publishing 18
Virona Publishing 21

Walpole, Horace 7, 11, 74
Walsh, Jill Paton 22-3
Ward, Philip and Audrey 17, 25-6, 49,
68, 81, 139
Warpole, Ken 113, 137
Waterstone's 14, 24, 83, 98, 99, 124
Wells, Gordon iv
Welsh Books Council 116, 136
where to raise the cash 28-31
Whitaker & Sons 36, 103, 110, 116
Whitaker's Almanack 131
Whitman, Walt 7
widows and orphans 62, 83
Wilcox, Ella Wheeler 12
Wild Hawthorn Press 22
Williams, Mogg 30
Williams, William Carlos 7, 12
Williamson, Hugh 81, 138
Wilshere, Sue iv
Winter Sweet 124
Woolf, Virginia 7, 11, 74
Word 46, 89
word counts 50-1
Worde, Wynkyn de 4
WordPerfect 46, 89
word processor 45, 46, 50, 69, 70, 72,
89, 92
World Wide Web 120-2
Writer's Companion 33
Writer's Handbook 29, 110, 125
Writers' & Artists' Yearbook 18, 29, 33,
35, 58, 110
Writers' Forum 22
Wynne-Tyson, Jon 113

Yale 81
Yeats, W. B. 12
Yellow Pages 56, 65, 84, 117